ᐱF422893

SIDE HUSTLE PODCAST

SIDE HUSTLE PODCAST

Build a One-Person, Million-Dollar
Business Podcasting from your
Living Room Couch

Alex Loudon

14662563 Canada Society
www.TheNaughtyLibrarian.ca

Copyright © 2026 by Alex Loudon

Published in the United States and globally by: 14662563 Canada Society
Project editor: 14662563 Canada Society Press Staff
Cover design: 14662563 Canada Society Press Design
Interior design and illustrations: 14662563 Canada Society Staff

All rights reserved. No part of this book may be reproduced by any mechanical, photographic, or electronic process, or in the form of a phonographic or digital recording, nor may it be stored in a retrieval system, transmitted, or otherwise be copied for public or private use—other than for "fair use" as brief quotations embodied in articles and reviews—without prior written permission of the publisher and author.

The author of this book does not dispense business mentorship advice or state the use of any business or entrepreneurial technique as a guaranteed form of success financial or otherwise. The intent of the author is only to offer information of a general nature to help you in your quest for understanding business success in podcasting and what has worked for the author and others recently. In the event you use any of the information in this book for yourself, the author and the publisher assume no responsibility for your actions.

Library of Congress Cataloging-in-Publication Data
Paperback ISBN: 979-8-218-87172-7
E-book, Audiobook: Direct on website.
10 9 8 7 6 5 4 3 2 1
1st edition, March 6, 2026
Printed in the United States of America.

This product uses responsibly sourced papers and/or recycled materials.

Disclosure And Legal

Disclaimer

This book is intended solely for educational purposes and does not constitute legal, business, financial, career, or investment advice. The content within this book is based on the author's research and personal experiences and should not be relied upon for making legal, business, financial, marketing, creative, or investment decisions or taking legal, business, financial, or investment actions on your behalf or on behalf of an organization. Readers are strongly encouraged to always consult with a competent attorney to obtain specific legal advice tailored to their individual circumstances and to always seek professional advice from qualified financial and investment advisors.

Furthermore, any business, financial, career, or investment advice provided in this book is for informational purposes only and does not guarantee any specific results. The author and publisher disclaim any liability for any losses or damages incurred due to applying the information contained in this book. Readers should perform their own due diligence and seek professional advice before making any business, financial, career, or other investment, creative or business decisions.

Investing in business entrepreneurship and creative ventures involves significant risks, including the potential loss of principal. The information provided here is for informational purposes only and should not be construed as financial, investment, career, creative, marketing or legal advice. Be sure to perform your own due diligence before making any investment, creative, or any other business decisions. Past performance is not indicative of future results. Past results of other podcasters does not guarantee new podcasters engaging in similar behavior will cause similar results. Always seek the counsel of a qualified financial advisor or other professional to determine the appropriateness of any investment strategy or transaction including entrepreneurial for your personal circumstances, but ultimately, any creative decisions, business choices and investments you make are made at your own risk.

This book may contain information on other websites and social media platforms and profiles operated by parties other than the author or the publisher. Such hyperlinks are provided for reference only. The author and the publisher do not control such websites, links and platforms and are not responsible for their content. The inclusion of such hyperlinks in the book does not necessarily imply any endorsement of the material on such websites or association with their operators.

"Once the flames begin to catch the wind
will blow it higher..."
Peter Gabriel

Contents

INTRODUCTION
Once Upon My Podcast

I want to be a mermaid.

It was December, California, 2024, just before the great fires that would eliminate the Palisades as it had always been known. I was walking on the beach looking out at the ocean. Day five. I couldn't shake the weight in my chest, the heaviness enveloping me like an oversized coat, causing it to be a struggle to breathe. I wanted to walk into the ocean. Just walk in. Like a mermaid.

Always resilient, I'd just completed my MBA and was renting a beautiful beach house to relax. With a friend in her 34th year of fighting Parkinson's disease and her light fading rapidly, we were doing a lot of hot tub therapy, watching sunsets, and giggling about everything, but it wasn't working. She was almost gone, and I wasn't bouncing back.

I'd had businesses do well over the years and others not so well. When something didn't work, I'd start something else. With my overpriced MBA completed, I was ready for my home run business. This one was not it. Again. Not quite. I had thrown my remaining resources into.

It was even on my vehicle license plate, the website name. I was all in. As usual.

Refusing to accept the reality of a non-visible disability which rendered my body largely useless and attacked me regularly with debilitating pain (and with some doctors telling me it would never go away and it was 'in my head' – no dilettante: I ran marathons and chased down bad guys–if I could wipe my own ass and tie my shoelaces right now pain-free, I would. It is in my hands, feet, and torso…jerk). My resilience was as strong as my physique. If the basement of rock bottom had a crawl space, my life was in it. Albeit with a good view, and some bubbles.

Mermaid life awaited.

I didn't. It's just not me. I'll take it to the miserable end because I love life. Thankfully my best friend on the other coast stuck by me, as always, during those five-hour conversations when the cobwebs just wouldn't clear. Ah, friendship.

I love technology, and have always been a geek, (but with great fashion sense). I love stories and books, and have written a few. I love being creative and adore artistic people from all areas of expression and their contributions to our shared experience. For fun I folded in with a dynamic group of local area writers as a diversion from the monotony of figuring my life out, again. ("Is there a do over?" "First positions, back to ones, with hindsight and feeling this time, everyone.") So a funny thing happened on the way to shelving an idea, giving up on entrepreneurism forever, and considering taking an extended swim. Not unlike when I figured out Picasso, and I mean really figured out his style, that naughty brat, by just staring at one of his works for an extended amount of time, mostly because I was stuck in place in general thought and was hitting the pause button for my tired feet adventuring through beautiful Paris museums while it happened to be in front of me.

My writing group friends said they thought my book podcast was a great idea. I thought the book was dead tbh but listened to them talk and since I had no direction I decided to just hammer out the idea for giggles on those warm Los Angeles Tuesday nights at 'group' over maté lattes. There was mention of the up-coming Los Angeles Festival of Books and some were going, taking a few bookmarks touting what they were doing. So with one episode of my new book podcast launched for fun, no hope left, a body that felt like shit, a spirit that felt worse, and a few paper bookmarks I ventured forth on a miserably rainy day in the land where dreams come true and it never rains. I went to the Los Angeles Festival of Books.

And in this la la land of happy endings I have always loved (I was one of the many hopefuls sitting in sweats with my besties, a chip bowl and an up-do each awards season culminating in the pinnacle where we all dressed long gown and white tie for the crescendo–hello to the "Oscars!"), something magical happened. It grew like a Canadian snowball racing down a hill searching for a fresh cherub face. On its own. With zero effort to make it a thing and no marketing budget outside of those initial flimsy black and white bookmarks. With absolutely no hustling, no begging family and friends to like it and tell others about it. All word of mouth. Wom. Wow. Strangers liking, following. Listening. Reposting. Only a few. But total and complete strangers. In many places in the world. OMG.

And, not knowing what I was doing, still, I reached out to a celebrity and asked him to be on the show. He had just put out his most recent book, had a well-known brother, and I thought his bravery in his life journey was incredible. Mr. Brian Cuban. The fiction, crime-thriller writer and body aware, recovering from addiction, and positive role model for others Brian Cuban.

Yes.

What? Yes? He said yes?? OK. I still don't know what I am doing but I'll record this one, I decided. So I did. It went great. Timing!

I kept wanting to shelf the project. I really did. Then something amazing would happen every time I wanted to stop. One guest after another seemed to gravitate toward me effortlessly, like they were being sucked into my vortex, my magnet. It was so inspirational and so much fun I just kept going. One more episode for the pleasure of it all. Why not? What else am I doing? It was a lot of work and learning but effortless in the details as they unfolded for me, as if the entire script was fully written for me and I just had to show up to take the step and the next step was there. Very Hollywood. Lovin' it.

It grew. It expanded. Listeners in more cities. Listeners in more countries! Bangladesh. Really? In Bangladesh? Spain. The UK. Other countries. Really. Can't be. It is. Really? In the first year so far, as this book takes shape there are listeners in over 23 countries and 153 cities, there are advertisers buying ads directly from me for commercials and embedded spots on episodes, there are bestselling authors and Pulitzer Prize-winning authors who have appeared as guests on episodes, there are world leaders, business leaders, millionaires, billionaires, and amazing people globally from all walks of life finding me on my main platform (LinkedIn, oddly–and nowhere else–more on that later because it is incredibly relevant for success–and not in obvious ways). They are connecting with me, listening and liking the show.

It continues to grow like wildfire. It wasn't supposed to be a thing. It was becoming a huge thing.

I liked the part about getting paid. Selling ads immediately when reaching out to strangers was a pretty amazing feeling. The sweet spot already? It certainly wasn't supposed to become a paying gig, or a career, or a business that would expand and thrive.

It did become all of that and more.

So are the humble beginnings of what continues to grow. SMH.

"Why would anyone listen to this thing?" I asked my friend, Friend 1.

"People watch golf, Allie," he said.

"So I said to Friend 1, why would anyone watch and listen to my podcast about authors of books and their stories, and he said 'people watch golf, Allie," I told Friend 2.

Friend 2 replies: "I watch golf." And I couldn't beat that logic.

It is now in its second year, seasons 3 and 4. We have advertisers approaching us. We receive "yes" answers when approaching the world's best writers to guest appear on the show. People keep asking me how I did it. ("Do you watch golf?") I wonder. I still don't really know. I just showed up, being me, setting it up the way my business mind thought made the most sense in the new frontier of direct-to-consumer content in the entertainment industry. (If there was money to be made from it I wanted it to go to me and my student loans, not some hoodie billionaire, so I ensured the set up from that first microphone moment would do just that: something this book will clearly share with you so you can, too!) Doing my best, not giving up, and having an indescribable amount of fun, my podcast show called The Naughty Librarian™™ "TNL" about storytellers and the stories they tell became a global hit.

So essentially, I've become an accidental influencer. Podcasters are the new rock stars apparently. And there is money to be made in this arena. Delicious money that pays the bills. Hundreds of thousands of dollars to millions and more for those who want to stick it out and be brave, after only a few years or less. From the comfort of your own living room couch in Boise or Cape Town, Albuquerque or Regina, Saskatchewan, or Llanfairpwllgwyngyllgogerychwyrndrobwllllantysiliogogogoch in Wales (that is a real place, 5 hours driving on the other side of the road from London, UK, and my friends from Wales are kind enough to never ask me to pronounce it...). Anywhere on the globe where there is an internet connection the show is available and people are learning about it, searching for it, and are listening to it.

Maybe you want to become a mermaid?

Maybe you are in your twenties and hate living at home but can't find a job? Maybe you are like 1 in 3 people in America who does not have $500 saved for an emergency and their current savings wouldn't help if they lost their job today.[1] Maybe you are like the public school teacher in America I spoke with this morning who is worried about how to pay for her constantly increasing heating bills because she is not due a raise for another ten years!

Maybe you are searching for your mermaid surfboard because you are part of a small business that is financially unsteady and at risk of failing like the myriad other ones that have recently gone over the cliff into demise? Data show US corporate bankruptcies are currently at a 15 year high.[2] Possibly you are looking to do something else at your company to increase revenue and avoid becoming the next business failure statistic, searching for that other way to take your profits from subzero to hero?

Maybe you are a student saving for college or university and do not want a mountain of debt just to get the education you need for the career you have chosen and don't feel like getting naked on another social

1   The Safety Net: Americans have $500 in emergency savings. (n.d.-b). Empower. https://www.empower.com/the-currency/money/safety-net-emergency-savings-research

2   US corporate bankruptcies set to hit 15-year high amid credit jitters, S&P data shows. (2025, November 13). www.reuters.com. Retrieved March 4, 2026, from https://www.reuters.com/legal/litigation/us-corporate-bankruptcies-set-hit-15-year-high-amid-credit-jitters-sp-data-shows-2025-11-13/

media platform to make some money to cover tuition? Possibly you are a stay-at-home parent seeking a money making opportunity that can work around your schedule and can help the family budget?

Maybe you have been in prison and can't find someone to take a chance on you and you want to be an earning, contributing member of society now instead of stealing for your next meal? Hello microphone! People love crime and prison stories. You have a great podcasting opportunity ahead of you.

Or maybe you are one of the millions of people in the lower half of the 'K shaped economy' just trying to make rent and buy groceries (a lovely word when you can afford them)? Perhaps you have already been laid off, let go, downsized, restructured, role-changed, rightsized, given your cardboard box and shown the door like those hard-working folks from Amazon (30,000 people in a recent wave of removals,[3] followed shortly after by another 16,000[4]), Microsoft, Intel and other technology giants (100,000 recently[5]), or Verizon (hanging up on about 15,000 humans[6]), or UPS (only 48,000 people this time[7]) for some recent examples. There are so many. Maybe you are concerned about losing your job be-

3   Bensinger, G. (2025, October 28). Exclusive: Amazon targets as many as 30,000 corporate job cuts, sources say. www.reuters.com. Retrieved March 4, 2026, from https://www.reuters.com/business/world-at-work/amazon-targets-many-30000-corporate-job-cuts-sources-say-2025-10-27/

4   Day, M., & Soper, S. (2026, January 28). Amazon to Cut 16,000 Corporate Positions to Trim Beaurocracy. www.bloomberg.com. Retrieved March 4, 2026, from https://www.bloomberg.com/news/articles/2026-01-28/amazon-to-cut-16-000-jobs-trimming-bureaucracy-amid-ai-tussle?embedded-checkout=true

5   Gupta, H. (2025, November 1). 100,000+ tech layoffs in 2025: Amazon, Microsoft, Intel, and these companies cut thousands of jobs. The Times of India. https://timesofindia.indiatimes.com/technology/tech-news%20/100000-tech-layoffs-in-2025-amazon-microsoft-intel-and-these-companies-cut-thousands-of-jobs/articleshow/125015287.cms

6   Shepardson, D., & Varghese, H. (2025, November 13). Verizon to cut about 15,000 jobs as new CEO restructures, source says. www.reuters.com. Retrieved March 4, 2026, from https://www.reuters.com/business/verizon-cut-about-15000-jobs-wsj-reports-2025-11-13/

7   Chapman, M. (2025, October 28). UPS cuts 48,000 jobs in the year to date as its turnaround continues | AP News. AP News. https://apnews.com/article/ups-amazon-layoffs-turnaround-85afc1c459883f41a2283c8394ce1eaf

cause you are hearing about all of these layoffs everywhere and you know companies are not loyal to employees any more?

In a year or two when the AI data centers get fully built out (much to the chagrin of those who love farm land in beautiful Michigan, Wisconsin and in other stunningly visual places where they are being built[8]) then the real bleeding will begin because although companies in all industries have started to replace people with artificial intelligence and a digital labor force (something those with jobs call 'efficiencies' and 'increased productivity') once those data centers are fully built out the people who used to do the jobs that AI will now do will also be irrelevant, not needed, unnecessary, pick your preferred term for your digital twin replacing you in the cube farm who does not even need an empty soda bottle for a bathroom break. Then that tsunami of real and permanent job losses will plow to our shores.

You do not want to be in the path of this wave. You know this.

Maybe you are just tired of never having quite enough money to live life as you hear about your friends' recent cruise or new car that doesn't have tape on it?

It could be that you have been podcasting for a while and have not made money doing so but have heard about others who have and are curious about how you can as well? Possibly you have a huge social media following somewhere and want to monetize it with a new revenue stream like a podcast but do not know where to start? Or maybe you just want to be like Cartman on South Park and have your own podcast because it is pretty awesome? Blame Trey and Matt!

Whatever your reason, you are looking at this book because you are curious about how to effectively start a side hustle podcast to make extra money while having some fun. In this book I will teach you about this easy opportunity to start earning money podcasting without spending a lot to get started or having to relocate to do it.

In its first year, with four months between seasons, my surprise, smash hit podcast The Naughty Librarian™ "TNL" exploded with listeners and financial success. The podcast achieved a 9,999,900% annual listener growth rate, 14,900% city listener growth increase, 2,200% country

---

8   A $15 billion data center prompts a small town reckoning near Lake Michigan. (2025, November 17). https://nextcity.org/urbanist-news/a-15-billion-data-center-prompts-a-small-town-reckoning-near-lake-michigan

listener growth increase, it charted at #134 on Apple Podcasts ahead of my friends at TMZ, and attracted advertisers directly–entirely through word of mouth, without spending a single dollar on marketing. Those are results a side hustle stays up at night dreaming of. The formula for this success is what I will share with you in this book.

Side Hustle Podcast is the definitive guide to podcasting as a business, offering practical, actionable information and steps to grow a global audience and generate revenue—even with no prior experience. Written by a Small Business Administration (SBA) award-winning MBA and entrepreneur who has achieved rapid podcasting success, this book reveals a proven formula with insider tips and little-known strategies that no other resource on the subject freely shares. Unlike generic guides that focus on technical details or offer casual entertainment, Side Hustle Podcast equips you to launch, scale, and monetize your podcast from day one, giving you a clear roadmap to build and grow a profitable podcast business. In these pages, I'll show you exactly what I did and how you can repeat what I did to achieve the same or even greater success. This isn't luck; it's strategy and consistency. In these pages you'll discover what others won't tell you, giving you the inside track to podcasting success.

This isn't theory—these are proven tactics that work. You'll learn everything you need to start and grow a profitable side-hustle podcast, with the potential to generate real wealth. It includes an actionable workbook in the last chapter listing goals and key steps to take to launch and grow your own podcasting business.

While this book is not technical it introduces and explains many relevant, important business, podcasting, and entertainment industry concepts so you are savvy and equipped with the proper language as you grow your podcasting empire and count your profits. You can literally start with zero knowledge and experience about either business or podcasting and learn everything you need to know to get on your path to side hustle podcasting success with this book.

Welcome to your new, wonderful life. This entrepreneurial journey you are about to embark on costs almost nothing to start and because of the way I did it I made the money, not some hoodie clad technology titan who does not blink on whose platform I uploaded my free content to so they could make money off of my work as they kept laying off their loyal employees. They are not using me. I am using them. There are subtle yet important differences in how you should set up your podcast as a business right from the start to have this structure work for you as well. These secrets are shared in this book.

But wait, you say…I'm not dancing in a crop top on ClickTock with a million followers? I'm too old. I am seriously underwhelming on social media. The good news is that you do not need to already have a following anywhere or to be a celebrity to get started and have success as a podcaster. I didn't. Many other successful podcasters didn't. Gone are the days when teenage teetees in a tank top and mansplaining manosphere musings are what get you to the top of the podcast charts and multi-million dollar podcast deals (both done to death). There is a lot of room for every other person, style, and voice. Like anything else in life, being you is your best option, not imitating someone else, successful or otherwise.

Much like the early days of television and motion pictures, the web, or apps, there is so much uncharted, untried creative territory in podcasting it is wide open for you to get in and earn your piece of success. People watch golf, friends. People watch golf.

Remember, the product you are giving to the listeners of your podcast is absolutely free to them. Free is something people globally can get in on, and do. Their free listening drives your money making, which is the revenue model and formula that will be explained in this book.

People–especially young adults and new graduates entering the workforce now are stuck in a "no-hire" job market and a stagnating global economy where opportunities to earn a solid, honest paycheck are dwindling and good people are literally debating a life of crime to feed their families. Why not try it? (Your first side hustle, not the crime path.) From the comfort of your living room couch. With a few hundred dollars, a few hours a week, a light bulb idea and this book. Your couch should have a seatbelt because it is about to soar!

Most podcasters pay less than $50 a month to podcast and put out as many episodes as they like. A few dollars a day essentially gets you started and that's a heck of a lot less than what my MBA cost me so I could emerge as the most overqualified kiddie day care shuttle driver ever (truth–before the podcast hit).

Like I used to say to the young, dumb broke public high school kids I taught business to in America between bloodied fist fights in class before they were carted off to suspension: 'make a good choice'. Rather than cheat and steal, consider becoming an entrepreneur. Be the boss, baby. Build it and get yours. Side hustle your way to financial success with your very own podcast. When you earn it honestly like this, you get to keep it.

You can't win if you are not in it. Time to get in the game. Literally anyone from anywhere can have, and host a podcast.

When I asked AI what career I could choose and listed my specific symptoms and challenges that made it difficult to impossible to hold down one of those great, full-time jobs people are happy to have before they get laid off from, this was the response, reproduced here verbatim:

Podcast Host or Producer

> You can create and host your own podcast or help produce others' podcasts. It's a highly creative role that requires minimal physical exertion and allows you to focus on content creation and discussion. Once established, podcasts can be monetized through sponsorships or advertising.

OK digital assistant. So noted. So done.

You, dear reader, can come from any walk of life, want to make money for any reason, and have any message you want to podcast out to the world. To be clear, there is no guarantee that your podcast will make money using this formula or any other one, but if you read this book and learn what I did and repeat it there is a real chance you can have the success you seek. This book has current, timely information no one else is sharing with you that works to grow and monetize a podcast without needing to spend thousands of dollars to enroll in a master class or a course on the subject to learn it.

Podcasting is the wild west right now, in its relative infancy, and changing rapidly. It is taking a slice of Hollywood and sending it from Des Moines or Ding Dong or anywhere else directly to the world. It is content and content is Queen and King globally, everywhere right now, no matter where you are from. You send it from your location and the world picks it up right where they are. Now is the time to jump into the hot tub, turn up the jets, throw in the crystals and beads and find out for yourself what's in you and what you can make of this golden opportunity.

In these pages you will learn about basic business, the industry of podcasting, and how it presents a goldmine of an opportunity for you right now. It tells you the way to set up from the start to enable effective monetization. It explains the basics about gear, branding, selecting your niche, and making, editing and launching episodes. It tells you how to build your team and protect your podcast and its intellectual property ('IP") with answers to the most current questions on the subject directly from a seasoned expert in the legal profession. It explains how to manage rejection and failure which is really a step on the path of success. It informs you on how to track and analyze your growth so you can obtain revenue from advertisers, partners, sponsors and more. It also suggests how to keep and grow your wealth once you obtain it with your successful podcast, and explains to you how to grow and scale the entire operation for even more success. Throughout, it uses my global hit podcast called The Naughty Librarian™ "TNL" as a real-world, current case study to elucidate the topics. We have walked our talk and now we share it with you here.

In this book you get the secrets that others are not telling you, either because they do not know or they do not want you to know because they would make less money off of you if you did. No guesswork is required. This book includes details about how to use the variety of platforms, networks and directories that currently exist and make them work for you rather than the other way around. You are no dummy. With the right information and a little effort, you can take this as far as you want.

New entrepreneurs line up. You are about to go to podcasting school. Swimming optional. Staying afloat, obviously. Bubbles everywhere you want them.

Mermaids need not apply.

Hi, I'm Alex. I'm The Naughty Librarian™ "TNL". Nice to meet you Naughty Brats! Now, tell me your podcast story…

CHAPTER 1
The Podcast Goldmine
Video Podcasting is the Now and Next Frontier

Podcasting is a nascent industry. Like gladiators fighting for survival, it is finding its way with virtually no rules. It transcends country borders. It has no central authority it must answer to. Glorious anarchy! It is loosely made up of several social media platforms, directories, networks, and other related technologies and activities. To the victors will go both the spoils and the badge for figuring out the structural foundation for others to follow because when something works it is repeated by those who also want the same success. One of those winners can be you.

Podcasting didn't start with Hollywood studios or stars—it began with a tinkerer's spark. For geeky history buffs, here is a short summary of what got us all to this point. Those who find history boring can skip this short yet interesting section which provides important foundational context. Those who are curious, read on.

In the early 2000s, developer Dave Winer slipped an "<enclosure>" tag into RSS, letting audio files hitch a ride on web feeds—a move scholars mark as podcasting's technical birth.[1] Happy birthday to us! In 2001 he even posted a Grateful Dead track this way,[2] while researchers at Harvard's Berkman Center explored "audioblogging" as a new digital storytelling frontier.[3] It was messy, clever, and unexpectedly full of life. This new area of work meets play.

In 2004, journalist Ben Hammersley named it—"podcasting"[4] (thank you for not naming it "Hammersley-ing, for obvious reasons) and then Apple's 2005 iTunes update sent the new medium soaring.[5] Steve Jobs (essentially, a dead guy everyone wants to emulate at annual business conventions and who is the reason you never get off your Apple phone or use it to actually talk with anyone–the co-founder of a little company made big called Apple Inc.) pushed it as "the next generation of radio," and a "Wayne's World" type of space where anyone could broadcast to the globe.[6] Homemade, grassroots shows started to grow like weeds and people were getting the buzz. Or buzzed.

Scholars now describe podcasting as a hybrid medium—part radio, part participatory culture, part something entirely new.[7] From what we at the hit podcast The Naughty Librarian™ "TNL" are seeing, it seems to be a reemergence and synergistic mixing of old mediums meeting new

1   Wikipedia contributors. (2025, October 22). Dave Winer. Wikipedia. https://en.wikipedia.org/wiki/Dave_Winer

2   Nuzum, E. (2023, January 31). The story of the first podcast feed. Podnews. https://podnews.net/article/first-podcast-feed-history

3   Quirk, V. (2015, December 17). Guide to Podcasting. https://towcenter.columbia.edu/. Retrieved March 5, 2026, from https://towcenter.columbia.edu/news/guide-podcasting

4   Pew Research Center. (2024, April 14). What is Podcasting? https://www.pewresearch.org/journalism/2006/07/19/what-is-podcasting/

5   Apple. (2026, February 26). Apple takes podcasting mainstream. Apple Newsroom. https://www.apple.com/newsroom/2005/06/28Apple-Takes-Podcasting-Mainstream/

6   Contributors to Wikimedia projects. (2005, May 23). Apple Computer CEO Steve Jobs gives opening keynote to WWDC 2005. Wikinews, the Free News Source. https://en.wikinews.org/wiki/Apple_Computer_CEO_Steve_Jobs_gives_opening_keynote_to_WWDC_2005#:~:text=Apple%20Computer%20CEO%20and%20co,be%20soon%20available%20for%20Windows.

7   Bonini, T. (2022). Podcasting as a hybrid cultural form between old and new media (CC BY-SA 4.0). ResearchGate. Retrieved March 5, 2026, from https://www.researchgate.net/publication/358978959_Podcasting_as_a_hybrid_cultural_form_between_old_and_new_media_pre-print

ones, of the old school way of media turning into a new school way. It is a full-circle moment taking us all back to the pre-television days of radio when a family would gather round the large, brown radio in the living room each evening to listen to news, detective stories or other suspense filled adventures. Pre-television radio shows were developed in the 1910s and early 1920s and blossomed throughout the 1920s into the 1930s and 1940s because radios became affordable household items and broadcasters and advertisers created compelling entertainment and news programming that drew mass audiences before TV existed. It was called the "Golden Age of American Radio."[8]

Circles have a way of repeating and completing as the motion of history moves forward, with pie in the sky dreams leading technological revolutions. Sure, it is a hundred years later and people have purple hair and nose rings, but otherwise, the more stuff changes the more it remains the same and podcasts are the new radio shows. Welcome to the "Golden Age of Podcasting!" A goldmine moment for some.

Whatever it is and however it gets described, podcasting at present offers an opportunity for fame and wealth that is mammoth in size and growing and the important part of that you need to understand is that it is now big enough and developed enough so that you can get a piece as well. You can get in the game with a new podcast and make some money doing it. The rise of podcasting to its present state reflects shifting technology, listener habits, and the classic pull of personal, relatable storytelling. Everyone likes a good story.

What is the story of podcasting, by the numbers?

In a business plan, the "Market Analysis" section describes these numbers. It details the industry and the size of the opportunity being considered by an entrepreneur to show there is a demand for the business. Usually they need to pull this information together to determine if a business idea is viable. Here, I summarize and simplify this for you. (Spoiler alert: podcasting is viable, big time!)

This analysis involves something known as "TAM." TAM is not your friend Tammy, but it can be your friend if it is big enough. It is a business term that stands for the "Total Addressable Market" which is

---

8   Golden Age of American radio. (n.d.). https://www.britannica.com/. Retrieved March 5, 2026, from https://www.britannica.com/topic/Golden-Age-of-American-radio

business geek talk for how big the global mall is filled with your customers. TAM specifically tells the maximum revenue opportunity if the company captured 100% of its market share. It needs to be large enough for you to make money doing the activity, which in this case is podcasting and selling ads. If there are not enough customers buying your widget or whatever you are selling you will have a tough time making sufficient sales at any price to turn a profit and make your entrepreneurial venture worthwhile. That is why everyone wants to know what TAM is. This market is, whether we are looking at more conservative estimates or the larger ones.

Podcasting Industry Size & Dynamics (TAM)

What is the TAM for podcasting and, thus, this opportunity for you?

The podcasting industry covers audio and increasingly video-more on that later as it is critical to how you set yourself up for financial success. Podcasting is part of the digital media and audio entertainment industry. The industry intersects with streaming platforms, social media, and emerging audio-visual formats, making it both a content creation and technology-driven market. And you thought it was just a fun, little thing on your phone!

The podcasting industry has been valued to be a USD $7.3 billion industry in 2024[9] and in 2025 around USD $32.54 billion[10] or as much as USD $35.7 billion[11] with direct ad revenue as the main driver. It is a substantial and rapidly expanding segment of the digital media ecosystem. Podcasting itself has become a mainstream entertainment industry choice for some years now with others valuing it to be worth as much as USD $30 billion back in 2022 with about a third of that revenue from rapidly

---

9   The Global Podcast Economy: A Complete Picture. (n.d.). https://www. owlandco.com/insights/the-global-podcast-economy-a-complete-picture

10   Coherent Market Insights. (2025, April 9). Podcasting market size to worth USD 173.49 billion by 2032, says Coherent Market Insights. Globe-Newswire. https://www.coherentmarketinsights.com/insight/request-sample/4283

11   Future Market Insights. (2025). Podcasting market size and share forecast outlook 2025 to 2035. https://www. futuremarketinsights. com/reports/podcasting-market

growing advertising.[12]

The North American podcasting market is projected to expand to USD $65.76 billion by 2033, at a Combined Annual Growth Rate (CAGR) of 22.55%. Some say the market size of podcasting could be worth as much as USD $173.49 Billion by 2032![13]

What this means for you is that there is a massive opportunity for you to make money as a podcaster in the entertainment industry and sell advertisements on your episodes and other products and services, and this gold rush is growing. You do not need to move to Hollywood to do it either. More people everywhere will continue to consume digital content including podcasts, and more people can continue to produce and release podcasts from the comfort of home. All this will become easier for consumers and creators. Someone has to have a hit. I did. Why not you next?

Listening to podcasts drives the podcast's revenue. Where are these listeners geographically? Multiple sources suggest there are 584.1 million podcast listeners worldwide and approximately 158 million monthly listeners in the U.S.[14][15]   It has been reported that about 73% of Americans aged 12+ have consumed a podcast (listened to and/or watched) and about 55% of Americans are now monthly podcast consumers, meaning more than half the population in the USA regularly listens to shows.

The U.S. is the market leader, followed closely by Canada and Mexico, especially due to localized content. Platforms are expanding how

12   Statista. (n.d.). Entertainment - Worldwide | Statista market forecast. https://www.statista.com/outlook/amo/app/%20entertainment/world-wide?currency=USD#revenue_656542

13   GlobeNewswire. (2025, April 9). Podcasting market size to worth USD 173.49 billion by 2032, says Coherent Market Insights. GlobeNewswire. https://www.globenewswire. com/news-release/2025/04/09/3058669/0/en/Podcasting-Market-size-to-worth-USD-173-49-Billion-by-2032-says-Coher-ent-Market-Insights.html

14   RSS.com. (2025, October 17). Podcast statistics: The current state of podcasting. RSS.com. https://rss.com /blog/the-current-state-of-podcasting/

15   Podcast statistics and trends report. (2026). SoundCamps. Retrieved January 30, 2026, fromhttps://www.apple.com/ newsroom/ 2026/01/ 2025-marked-a-record-breaking-year-for-apple-services/

they make money on content uploaded by content creators and people like me are successfully figuring out how to use them and earn our own advertising revenue. The entire market is thriving with excitement, competition, and with diverse content and monetization opportunities. In short, podcasting is a digital gold rush (my term, you can use it, just credit me for saying it).

Like the rush for physical gold, that fevered moment in history when fortunes were gambled and sweat poured resulting in clear winners, hope gleams bright in this digital gold rush era as well with people from all walks of life able to get in the game and shoot their shot.

With about 4.5 million podcasts cataloged in the entire world as of late 2025–which is already a relatively small number when you are tapping in to a rapidly growing and changing global market like this one (think TV or movies in the early days–that potential), there are actually only about 500,000 people at the absolute most actually dropping new episodes regularly with the rest just dropping the entire idea of doing them altogether. These ones that have stopped producing and launching more episodes for any reason are known in the industry as 'dormant' podcasts. They have "podfade" which is when a podcast suddenly stops releasing new content without a final show or an announcement. [With The Naughty Librarian™ "TNL" we take time off between seasons and have 2 seasons a year, and this is not giving up or podfade. Repeat and new listeners return for each new season. Thank you!]

Any given lottery where it is advertised that millions of dollars can be won have odds in the area of 1 in 300 million of winning, give or take some millions. It is pretty hopeless to win but each week people 'play' the lottery. The odds of being struck by lightning in your lifetime should you live at least 80 years or so are much better (sorry) at 1 in just 15,300.[16] The odds of having a hit Side Hustle Podcast that makes you money if you set it up the way we suggest are somewhere between these two realities since I have not won the lottery or been struck by lightning, but I have hit on the formula to make money podcasting, and in my first year of doing so. The demand is so great and the supply (number of creators upload-

---

16   Hand, D. J. (2014). The improbability principle: Why coincidences, miracles, and rare events happen every day. Farrar, Straus and Giroux/Scientific American.

ing new shows and episodes–new content) is so relatively small the odds were in my favor. People who like podcasts are always looking for more content, more new shows they like. Interestingly, the odds of me getting a world renowned odds expert, statistician and bestselling author as a guest on my hit podcast to talk about these probabilities and more were not bad at all, and he said yes (episode in Season 3).

In just one month, October 2025, there were over 700 million hours of podcasts watched on YouTube[17] and now YouTube has over 1 billion monthly viewers for podcast content worldwide.[18] In 2025, approximately 584 million people listened to podcasts. Spotify held about 37% of the global podcast audience share, which implies that around 216 million people listened to podcasts on Spotify in 2025 (0.37 × 584 million ≈ 216 million).[19] Apple itself does not publicly report how many Apple Podcasts listeners it has. But it has said that 2025 was a record year for listener engagement, plays, and subscribers on the platform.[20] Others have estimated Apple Podcast listeners to be around 28.7 million in the USA in 2024.[21] These data suggest there is a very large crowd of listeners driving revenue at this mall. In total, there are a lot of people globally who are listening to podcasts. This is the demand part of the equation.

YouTube said it paid more than $100 billion to content creators in a four year span from 2021.[22] Yet not even a quarter of one percent

17   The YouTube Team. (2025, December 18). How podcasts took over the living room in 2025. YouTube Official Blog. https://blog.YouTube/news-and-events/podcasts-living-room-in-2025/

18   Katz, T. [Vice President, Partnerships, Podcasts]. (2025, February 26). Drop the Mic: celebrating 1 billion monthly podcast users on YouTube. Https://Blog.Youtube/. Retrieved March 6, 2026, from https://blog.youtube/news-and-events/1-billion-monthly-podcast-users/?utm_source=keywordsnippet&utm_medium=referral

19   Podcast statistics and trends report. (2026). SoundCamps. Retrieved January 30, 2026, from https://soundcamps.com/ blog/spotify-statistics/

20   Apple. (2026, January 12). 2025 marked a record-breaking year for Apple services. Apple Newsroom. https://www.apple.com/newsroom/2026/01/2025-marked-a-record-breaking-year-for-apple-services/

21   eMarketer. (2024). Podcast industry report: Apple Podcasts listeners (estimated 28.7 million U.S. listeners). Retrieved from https://www.emarketer.com/learningcenter/guides/the-podcast-industry-report-statistics/

22   Vallese, Z. (2025, September 16). YouTube says it has paid creators more than $100 billion since 2021. CNBC. https://www.cnbc.com/2025/09/16/YouTube-creators-pay.html

of all of its creators ever saw so much as a penny for all of the uploading of content they gave them.[23] Spotify paid out $100 million in 2025 revealing those details for the first time publicly without providing a breakdown,[24] yet most of the payments only went to 'top-tier' contributors. It was not spread evenly to all podcasters who uploaded their show episodes on their platform. Apple is apple and does not reveal any of these numbers, but the general story is likely similar. This is the 'you not getting paid' part of the equation if you do it the way they tell you to and hand them your content.

Clearly the market analysis shows the desire to consume podcasts is global and growing and there is enormous money to be made from podcasting and making revenue from successful shows. ***Who gets to make it and take it is determined by how you play the game.*** Hope is not a plan. Not knowing how it all works is a bad plan. Thinking the platforms will pay you after you become a success is not realistic and unlikely to lead to results, for most people.

I stumbled on a good way of doing this so I essentially cut myself in without needing their permission or waiting for a royalty check from them. I used those big platforms and managed to develop a revenue generation model immediately. I monetized from the first moment I uploaded my content everywhere. Really, I flipped the whole model on its back and made it work for me. I found the gold.

Now that you know the size of the opportunity and the market analysis suggests it is a feasible endeavor, and you want to get in the game with a side hustle podcast business, the foundational information you need to know to start a business that enables you to make money with your podcast will be detailed for all of you budding new entrepreneurs.

---

23   Made, M. (2023, November 20). Why less than 1% of YouTubers make money. Medium. https://medium.com/the-side- hustle-club/why-less-than-1-of-YouTubers-make-money-4dbb24db9edd

24   Testa, J. (2025, April). Spotify Has Paid More Than $100 Million to Podcasters to Take On Competitors. www.nytimes.com. Retrieved March 5, 2026, from https://www.nytimes.com/2025/04/28/business/dealbook/spotify-100-million-paid-creators-podcast-video.html

CHAPTER 2
Getting Started on Your First Million

Laying the Foundation From Idea to Business Plan

At tens of thousands of dollars per letter, I recently just completed a graduate-level professional degree focused on business management, finance, marketing, and leadership called an "MBA" which stands for Master of Business Administration (or 'miserable bank account' after paying for it). While it was supposed to equip freshly minted graduates with sought-after broad skills to get hired at a company in a number of industries and garner the corner office with a fast-track to a juicy six-figure salary, without connections to a wealthy parent or friend today it actually equips one with much less in the current state of the economy—one that is thriving only in the opinion of gaslighting politicians who want re-elected, those in the stock market who really are thriving, and those who have solid jobs they are hugging like a toddler to a blankie.

What this latest graduate degree really did for me, that I wanted it to, was it filled in the blanks of my mostly self-taught business knowledge. The school of experience had been good to me and I supplemented it with some fantastic business books and courses but I often wondered if I was missing anything significant additional business education could give me that life and books had not. I had done well in business with some six-figure deals and a few noteworthy accolades that provided me cool desk knick-knack trophies, including being awarded the prestigious Small Business Administration (SBA) Woman in Business Champion of the Year in 2011 for a company I founded and sold in Maryland, USA. No one was moving my cheese, but was it Appenzeller or Swiss with holes? I wanted to feel confident when I was running with my big home run idea that nothing would trip me up unexpectedly and sink the boat. As they say, you don't know what you don't know. I didn't know what I didn't know and I knew my MBA would give me the rest of what I knew I did not know. I thought.

An economics PhD who had never taken a business course or started a business in his life taught the "Business Plan" course. It was a good thing I had a ton of experience in the area already.

The contents in this chapter pull from knowledge that comes from my education and experience and is limited to what you need to know right away to get started with a side hustle business podcasting. It excludes a lot of academic theory you do not need that you can find elsewhere and add to your knowledge base later if you want to, so you can speak even fancier about it at trade shows and cocktail parties. For example, if you want to expound on your detailed mission statement and corresponding value statements learn about them and build them out in your business plan. You do not need to do this to pick a podcast topic, set up a business legally and launch episode one. Others might say you do. Ask to see their SBA award or where they got their MBA from, and if they can present those, listen if you want to.

Not wasting your time, I'm empowering you with immediate, actionable tools, providing you high-impact, information in a way that enables you to understand business sufficiently and get started immediately to be able to side hustle podcast to success.

You need a business plan to start. It is step one. Your business plan is a living document you can update and edit as needed. You should make a new one each new fiscal year. Remember nothing in this book is

intended to replace legal or other formal advice and you are encouraged
to do any additional learning you choose to supplement this lean, strategically targeted information provided to get you started immediately.

Your initial business plan will be unique. Each section should be
as long as it needs to be for you, and not longer. Only you know what exactly that looks like and it will be different for everyone. Nothing is set in
stone. Make changes and shuffle information as you like so it does what
you require it to. This information is a provided here in a logical order so
you do not need to make changes to it unless you want to when building
your first business plan. When you have filled in your information for
each of these key sections through your actionable workbook at the back
of this book you will be ready to start the business of podcasting.

Business Plan Key Components

Executive Summary
Company Description
Market Analysis
Organization and Management
Products and Services
Marketing and Sales Strategy
Financials
Appendices

Executive Summary

First, and this is very important, ignore the usual advice about
starting with the "Executive Summary" in a business plan. Don't write it
first. Over the years, I've learned that it's actually the worst place to start. It
drives high achievers bat crap crazy that it sits there empty as the first item
in a business plan document and takes until the end to complete. Leave it
there. The Executive Summary should be completed last because it's just
a summary of all the other finished sections. Don't remove it or move
it—you need it at the start once it's completed. For now, ignore it, finish
every other section first, and then return to it as the last step in making
your first business plan. Once filled in, it will sit proudly at the front where
it belongs.

Company Description

This section explains at an introductory level who you are, what you do, who you serve and with what, how you make money doing it, why you're different, and where you're going. Put your business name here, which may be the same or different from your name or your podcast name. Say where the business is located and introduce the legal structure it has (read the next section for guidance on this). In this section you can also outline the company's history, current stage of development, and the problem your business aims to solve (which can be as simple as giving people more great entertainment in your podcast they will not find anywhere else, or turning a large social media platform following into a money making podcast, as examples).

In this section you can introduce the way you intend to make money. To decide how you will monetize and generate revenue ask yourself what you want to sell to people and businesses along with your podcast episodes you are releasing free. It might be, for example, that you will sell pre-roll, mid-roll, or post-roll dynamically inserted host-read or client-provided advertisements in your podcast episodes, or you will get sponsors or partners, or sell merchandise. You can offer subscriptions and premium content with bonus episodes, early access, behind-the-scenes content, access to live events and more. How would you like to build the money making element of your podcast, keeping in mind your interests, talents and experience? Briefly outline this in the company description. Later sections of the business plan go into greater detail on the company.

Market Analysis

The "Market Analysis" is important for a business plan. This was done for you in the last chapter. It shows you the size of the opportunity for a business, which in this case is a side hustle podcast. If you want to condense the information from the last chapter and put it in this section of your business plan please do so. Just credit this book as a source if you are using it for anything scholastic or otherwise external in the world as required. As the last chapter outlined, the business idea of podcasting was validated. It represents a profitable opportunity to put your time and money into.

The "Organization and Management" section of a business plan typically describes the business's legal ownership structure in detail, the leadership team, key roles, and how the company is managed. It also includes general operations (at least until your company gets bigger and then that section can be broken out to be its own component of your larger, more detailed business plan). Tax, finance, licensing, and other business obligations can be outlined here.

Selecting your business structure is an important step in building any business. A discussion of this now follows.

Legal Business Structures

What legal structure do you want your business to have? You have to choose the legal structure of your business. This is critical to your success so it is being explained here in detail. Where and how you legally set up your business triggers more required activities like setting up (and annually reporting/paying) state and local taxes and federal taxes, other business/financial reports and accounts, possible licenses, and more. You may be limited on where you can set up a business based on your citizenship or residency status. This chapter focuses on people who are able to set up businesses based in the USA.

If you actually do nothing to formally and legally set up a business and just start podcasting and making money know that you are still making a choice about this (possibly a bad one) and you are still one legal type of business.

The short version concerning why you want to choose one type of formal business structure and set it up legally is because no matter how much you might make, you could lose it all because most legal business structures aim to protect those in business from being sued and losing all of their personal wealth and assets. It creates a barrier between you and the idiots who think a lawsuit is the ticket to their retirement account. Even if you win, after a long court battle you have spent your time and money dealing with it, so you lose. It is, therefore, wise to choose a business structure that benefits you by limiting your liability. At least be aware of this reality, or remain ignorant of it at your peril.

Common business structures in America include Sole Proprietorships, LLCs, C-corporations and S-corporations.[1] A brief summary of each with their pros and cons will be presented here. Note there are also other forms of businesses that can be established but these are the standard ones you'll probably choose from as a new podcaster since you don't have a dental degree and aren't planning to do brain surgery while you record your podcast episodes, I hope.

A Sole Proprietorship is the easiest and least expensive option, (and also the dumbest as I've tried to explain…not saying sole proprietors are dumb, they are not, they are amazing, but even current ones should reconsider how they are set up and think about updating and legally structuring to become something safer). To be a "sole prop" as it is sometimes referred to in short, requires little more than selling a product or service, and filing taxes for your business activity on a schedule with your regular personal tax return. You retain full control of your business but you also carry full personal liability for all debts and legal claims of the business, you may struggle to secure funding if you seek it, and your legal business name defaults to your own unless you legally file a "doing business as" aka DBA document and pay a fee with the right regulator.

A Limited Liability Company (LLC) gives you liability protection with far less paperwork than a corporation. Profits pass directly to you without having to complete another nasty tax return for the business each year–no separate corporate tax return needs to be filed. Members, however (you and your buddies if you go in together), must pay non-deductible self-employment taxes, are taxed on profits whether distributed or not, and you cannot pay yourselves regular wages. The "you make it, the IRS takes it" rule still applies (it always does).

Up next is something called a Corporation. There are different types of corporations. C-corporations specifically also provide liability protection and allow easier fundraising through stock sales, appeal to employees with broader benefits, and can retain earnings within the company. The trade-offs include double taxation on dividends and the burden of extensive formalities, filings, and governance requirements. That is pret-

---

1 Forester, D. (2019, February 19). Business structure: Which works best for you. SCORE. https://www.score.org/resource/blog-post/business-structure-which-works-best-you

ty big jargon for saying you can grow it bigger and make real bank but you have more annoying paperwork and other reporting requirements and your accountant's bill will probably be higher. Some do, some don't choose this type of legal setup. It's like wearing pearls on bare skin with your black cocktail dress. No one can tell you what to do and no one way is necessarily better than the other. They are just different.

Then there is something called an S-corporation and it is a bit like if an LLC and C-corporation had a baby, it would be an "S-Corp." Choosing to set up this legal structure gives you the blended features of LLCs and C-corporations, offering pass-through taxation and requiring owner-employees to take "reasonable" wages, which can reduce self-employment tax. But they face restrictions such as a 100-shareholder limit, U.S.-citizen ownership requirements, and only one class of stock, and they can draw more IRS scrutiny if wages and distributions are not well documented. Again, the accountant is making bank and there could be benefits to choosing this one. An S Corporation also provides the liability protection discussed above because it is a separate legal entity, so owners are generally not personally responsible for the business's debts or legal obligations.

Honestly, most people choose an LLC and register in some business friendly state where they have a lot less hassle than in most other states. It is easy, relatively painless, and usually cheaper. And it protects your assets from the vultures who would rather litigate you than earn it on their own to grow a fortune. Do some online searches to see which states are currently business friendly as this varies over time. In the past states like Delaware, Nevada, sometimes South Dakota, and a few others were the go-to states to set up a company. Everywhere else they are going to hassle you to death with poor set up, expensive reporting requirements and lousy service…allegedly.

Additional Set Up Requirements

Sometimes you need to add an extra step to set up your business legally if you do not live in the state you register your company in. Delaware, for example, solves this easily. You hire a business that serves as a "Registered Agent" in that state. There, a registered agent is required to accept service of process for your business (such as lawsuits), receive official legal notices, and help ensure the business maintains compliance with state law. Through them you file a report and pay a fee to the government annually (either on your own through them to the state, or they file it for you with the state and charge you more–you still have to do the work). Unless you want to burn some Benjamins just learn how to do it yourself through them as it is easier and a lot less expensive most of the time–I always did. It satisfies regulators as if you lived there. It makes your business "compliant" every year so you do not get suspended and shut down.

To be clear I am not specifically endorsing any one type of legal structure in any one location over any other. I personally have set up different types of companies in different countries, provinces, and states including in Delaware and Nevada in the USA. I have been happy with them both, Delaware especially.

Once you choose your legal business structure and file the appropriate documents and articles (articles of incorporation for a corporation, articles of organization or partnership agreements for others, and so on) after verifying that your business name is available, and registering it with the state you choose to be located in you also need to set up your business operation to satisfy the federal tax agency, which in the USA is the Internal Revenue Service (IRS), and any state and local tax departments. Federally, you apply to the IRS to get an Employee Identification Number (EIN) or Federal Employee Identification Number (FEIN) which is (surprisingly) free. An EIN and a FEIN are exactly the same thing. They both refer to the exact same nine-digit tax ID issued by the IRS to you to identify your business so they can milk your profits like a cow, but failing to pay your taxes properly because you think it is unfair or excessive creates more problems for you and they take the ribeye too, so it is our strong suggestion that you just accept it and do your best.

Unless you are doing a cash business you cannot and should not avoid the IRS. They say they even want to know about any cash you receive from any business activity everywhere, like I've seen many a local cash-only thrift shop or food truck or mom n pop operation in rural America do. If you go that route then that is between you and them. If you are podcasting you are public and you can't get away with "being cash." It's about as private as a pimple on your nose. Pretty much never.

Having helped low income people complete and file their taxes with IRS certification to do so for a number of years in several states, I can attest to the fact that as a sole proprietor the saying 'you make it they take it' is on steroids when it comes to the 95,000 plus page IRS tax code in America and the hard-working sole proprietor. You pay out more and keep less of the exact same dollars of profit by being a sole proprietor than you do other legal forms of business. That and the fact that someone can sue you for everything and take it all means it is a lousy option for practically everyone. Did I mention a sole prop is a terrible option?

Moving on to the next component you should have in this section of your business plan, you should indicate who is on the team. List management. It might be short and sweet. You. You. You. And maybe some friends? You can add a resume from anyone who is part of the company by referring to it here and putting it as an Appendix at the end of the document if you want to be really formal about it.

On Taxes and Bean Counters

Use reputable tax professionals. I do not personally recommend the name brand walk-ins with all of the commercials at tax time–I have seen countless people charged hundreds or thousands of dollars per return and have had their taxes done wrong. You are better off searching for a credentialled professional. In the USA credentials that commonly prepare and file business tax returns are CPA (Certified Public Accountant), EA (Enrolled Agent), and JD (Juris Doctor/Tax Attorney), with CPAs and EAs doing the majority of business tax work. CPAs (Certified Public Accountants) in the USA are not federally regulated. Rather, they are state-licensed professionals who provide accounting, tax, financial planning, and consulting services to individuals, businesses, and other organizations. Individual state boards of accountancy license and regulate them. They charge a lot, and you usually get what you pay for. Asking friends and people in your community can get you a good referral sometimes. This hired person is an important team member in your sphere and it is critical to choose well. List this important team player in your business plan.

In Canada, a CPA (Chartered Professional Accountant), or a Tax Lawyer (LLB or JD) prepares business tax returns for complex matters, and historically by legacy designations CA (Chartered Accountant), CGA

(Certified General Accountant), and CMA (Certified Management Accountant), which are now all smartly unified under the CPA designation. If you do not want to become a podcaster consider becoming a CPA in Canada because they are harder to find than a sunburn in January in Nunavut. I tried to get audited statements for months offering hundreds of dollars an hour one year without luck and lost a seed round because of it.

This brings up an important point. Governments want people to set up businesses so they can tax these businesses just like they do people (a business has 'personhood' in America and pays its own separate taxes). Because of this there might be some taxpayer funded free or low cost local support for entrepreneurs at every stage of a business, including at the start-up stage.

One nonprofit organization funded in part by taxpayer money that can be useful to you in the USA is SCORE[2] which is a 501(c)(3) organization and a resource partner of the U.S. Small Business Administration (SBA). It has the goal to help people like you, side hustle business people who want to learn more and do it right. This organization helps small businesses plan, launch, and grow. It has been around since 1964 and is a large volunteer network of expert business mentors, giving lots of free information and support and various resources to entrepreneurs. I have not worked for them or with them and they do not pay me to tell you about them but they have tended to be a solid resource over the years so they are getting a mention here. Their website has a lot of good information for entrepreneurs at all stages.

You can ask a friend or hire a corporate attorney if you feel you want the guidance to legally set up your business and corresponding related accounts properly. But it can all be done easily by most individuals not new to earth who can read and talk. I promise. Local libraries are also a wealth of free information and know of many other local sources that support budding entrepreneurs as well. Librarians are some of the best, kindest, most knowledgeable and helpful people around. (And talented, and naughty we hear…).

Some businesses also need to set up licenses or other operating permits depending on their geographical location and industry of operation. If your podcast is live on the street in some parts of California, for example, they may require you to have a vendor's license or other day

2   https://www.score.org/

production licenses. If you are small and shooting in an out of the way place or in your own home they are unlikely to notice but they want me to make sure you know that they want these fees from you.

Typically, most podcasts from the living room couch do not need any additional operating licenses from any federal, state or local organization. Yay! If you do require any additional licenses, list them in this section of your business plan as well. Creative content licenses, if required for your podcast content, are covered in a later chapter on Intellectual Property. You might need those depending on the podcast you are creating.

Keep images of the legal documents for all aspects of setting up your business in a digital folder in the cloud (there are lots of affordable cloud storage options). You will need them often over the years for different reasons. One is when you open a dedicated business bank account the first year. You will need to set up a business bank account to do business and cannot just use a personal account.

Every bank is different except in two ways. They all overcharge you with hefty fees when something goes wrong for you, and they will all need those documents you were sent when you legally formed your business to open a business bank account. Expect the process to take a few hours in the chair of the bank employee and thank money launderers for all the laws that make it a time-consuming, one-time set up activity. But it only happens once (or in my case, twice, when I did a mermaid pivot then changed the name on the bank account–but by that time I had 'bank power' that comes with connections and balances so I literally phoned it in, which is not common).

You need the business bank account set up and those documents to then set up the payment service provider (PSP) which is a third-party company like Square[3] that allows your business to accept electronic payments, such as credit card and debit card payments in person and on your website. Get your node in the nerd network friend to code these links into your website if you choose. It is easier now than it was. List your selections in your business plan and store the documentation you receive in the cloud. These choices are all part of what is called your 'tech stack' that you utilize in your business.

You should also keep a separate credit card for business use only if you can, even if it is a personal credit card for now until the business is

3	https://squareup.com

able to get one.

Set up bookkeeping or accounting software to track income and expenses immediately, the same day you register your business so you are not one of those shoe box people at the end of the year. Trust me, it saves you time, money and headaches each year at year-end. You can do these tasks yourself if you are so inclined and have the time and want to save money, or you can hire a bookkeeper right away. Whether you are digitally savvy or not, try to start all your activities including daily financial activities digitally and avoid paper. It just tends to be easier, faster and more cost-effective as the years roll on. List your choices in your business plan.

Put your regular obligations like filing reports and deadlines in your business plan so you know to meet your monthly, quarterly and annual obligations. You can have a 'Business Activities Calendar" spreadsheet by month, or a "Shit List" or a "Checklist" that has a daily, weekly, monthly, quarterly and annually items tab for each. Your style determines how you want this to look and you know the best way you work.

The Organization and Management section of your business plan contains the above critical information that, when set up, provides a strong foundation from which you can operate a podcast to make money.

Products and Services

What is being sold? Is a podcast a product or a service?

An actual podcast itself (the episodes, brand, feed, archives) is a media product—something packaged, consumed, and distributed globally. Listeners "buy in" with attention and in other ways that can be monetized. Like a book, or a film, it exists as intellectual property (IP) that can be controlled and monetized. See Chapter 4 for details on intellectual property.

You can also be selling related services once an audience is built up and people will buy them. Maybe you will choose to do online workshops people can register for and pay a fee for in advance? Maybe you want to give classes or lessons?

Revenue streams can include anything you can think of that people might want to buy that you can legally sell them and can include both products and services. You can sell advertisements, sponsorships, partnerships, courses, paid interviews, affiliate and lead connections, tickets to live events, merchandise ("merch"), a make-up line, behind-the-scenes (BTS) additional content through subscriptions, email keep ups, live streams, live events, newsletters, and more. The sky is the limit and you can choose.

As you develop your revenue streams, list those details into your business plan. You might start with just one, the main one most podcasters have to make money: advertisements. There is nothing wrong with that. It works for many companies. Then you can expand to selling other products and services as your podcast listenership grows if you like.

How much should it cost?

How much a business charges a customer, or pricing, is simple, really. Listeners get to listen to the podcast free everywhere podcasts are available. The pricing of whatever you have to sell starts wherever you like it to. Start small, when you are small, so you will get buyers who will take a chance on you. The cost can go up as you grow your following and demand increases for the limited supply.

Our very first ad we sold for a mere $25 on the agreement the terms were confidential. It enabled the second ad to be sold for much more and now nothing sells for less than $1,000, including a ten-second spot. If people are paying for it, you are pricing it right. If they are not, you might need to rethink the price point, or work harder on growing the demand for your podcast advertising spots. Future chapters go into greater detail explaining some ways successful podcasts can approach pricing advertisements based on audience size, the type and placement of the advertisements, and more.

Marketing and Sales Strategy

Your listeners and buyers of whatever you choose to sell are "target markets" and these groups can be segmented by demographics, interests, behaviors, and in other ways. These groups have similarities and the more narrow your niche podcast topic is the more similarities your listeners will have. Chapter 3 discusses your branding and niche in detail so for now know that whatever niche you choose you will have a specific group of people that will like it and will pay you for what you are selling, and you need to develop a marketing and sales strategy with tactics to find them.

For simplicity let's assume you are selecting a podcast topic by working backward and aiming for a group: you are an entomologist and your podcast will be for people who love insects. Insects are an abundant topic. Scientists do not know the exact number of insect species on Earth. There are so many, only a few have been formally described and named. There are about 1.5 million beetle species.[4] That is a lot of types of beetles…who knew? You are excited about the topic so you believe other people will be as well. Your enthusiasm will draw them to listen. Your podcast will be about insects and fly all around the topic, with a focus on beetles since there is so much rich information in that even more narrow niche. Your very first episode might be about how Starbucks once used a coloring called cochineal (beetle blood, crushed parasitic beetles), to make its red dyes used in their strawberry drinks, until the vegan crowd caught on: like a lot of makeup and fashion lines still do as well.[5] Beetlejuice and beyond!

You need to develop a 12 Month Marketing and Social Media Plan and Calendar for your podcast about bugs and beetles to promote it to attract listeners and advertisers. You put it in this section of your business plan. To do this, first you need to know some marketing basics. The next section gives you a crash course on the most important elements of marketing followed by a sample 30 Day Social Media Plan which can be repeated monthly along with the other marketing and promotional activities in your 12 Month Marketing and Social Media Plan.

Marketing Basics

Marketing is the overall strategy of identifying customer needs and creating, pricing, and delivering value. Promotion is the specific set of activities used to communicate and advertise that value to customers. Oftentimes people use the terms interchangeably however they are not the same. A social media post, for example, is part of a larger marketing strategy and is a promotional activity because it is a specific tactic used to

---

4   Wikipedia contributors. (2025b, October 23). Insect biodiversity. Wikipedia. https://en.wikipedia.org/wiki/Insect_biodiversity

5   Hsu, T. (2019, March 15). Starbucks to drop beetle juice from the menu - Los Angeles Times. Los Angeles Times. https://www.latimes.com/archives/la-xpm-2012-apr-19-la-fi-starbucks-bug-color-20120420-story.html

communicate and advertise a product or service to an audience.

Being strategic and keeping this information actionable and useful for you immediately, here are the marketing pillars required for a successful message of any form in any channel. Keep these in mind for all your promotional tactics.

▶ GRAB ATTENTION! You have about 3 to 7 seconds to capture the viewer's attention. Example: Watch and learn how a dung beetle can pull over 1,000 times its own weight! Why this works: it is not normal and people like odd, amazing facts. People watch golf. People regurgitate facts they learn elsewhere.

▶ Focus on the consumer, not you and stress the benefits. Example: Free entertainment and learning all in one place in our podcast available now! Why this works: you are not telling them what you want, which is for them to tune into your podcast. You are telling them what is in it for them if they do so and you are presenting it in a way that sounds appealing. People are always looking for what is in it for them. It's human nature.

▶ Stand out from the competition. Differentiate yourself from other podcasters. Example: Other podcasts that talk about bugs do not have an expert host and we do. Why this works: people seek what they believe to be credible sources. This ties into the next pillar required in every marketing message you send.

▶ Establish your credibility. Example: If you are a widely respected entomologist, say it! "I am one of the world's most respected entomologists, and they call me Dr. Bug Guy." Why it works: If you really are a PhD in the field you have earned your credibility and you are just letting people know. Credentials tell truths. I started this book by stating I was awarded the prestigious Small Business Administration Women in Business Champion of the Year and included one of my most recent business education credentials, an MBA. I listed the explosive growth my hit podcast The Naughty Librarian™ obtained in year one. These are observable metrics. They tell you I know business and grew a hit podcast. People gravitate toward what they believe are credible sources.

▶ Build real value for your audience. Example: We tell you how to spot and avoid the blood-red blister beetle because its poisonous blood will infect you if you encounter it at a picnic. Why this works: People like messages that help keep them alive and pain free. The cost-benefit to tuning in to your show and this information could be significant and worth doing so.

▶ ALWAYS ADD A CALL TO ACTION (CTA). Example: "This common spider will kill you and to avoid certain death after it bites you… hear the rest on the next episode of the podcast Dr. Bug Guy." Why this works: Anyone who wants to live and hear the rest of this sentence has to tune into the podcast to get the life-saving information. It indicates what you want them to do next, guiding their behavior. Always have a call-to-action in everything you communicate.

Obviously it can be clunky to literally have all pillars stand out in each and every short message everywhere but you want to aim to ensure all the elements are there as much as possible or are otherwise implied. As you implement the above tips into all of your marketing messages everywhere you will quickly see what works and will want to repeat it. This is how your marketing efforts will achieve results and you will grow your podcast for success.

With a focus on ensuring all communication has these marketing basics you need to develop a "12 Month Marketing Calendar" which includes a "30 Day Social Media Plan" you can repeat each month for the first year. The template here provides one example of a simple plan. Future chapters explain the concepts listed including branding, niche, and so on in more detail. For now put this in your business plan and you can add to it as you read that additional information and add to your plan.

12-Month Marketing Calendar Sample

Month 1 — Marketing & Podcast Setup
- Decide on your brand image, colors
- Pick your podcast niche, name & tagline
- Register domain name and begin building website for the podcast
- Create podcast logo and related graphics including placeholders
- Set up social media accounts and channels (Instagram, TikTok, Bluesky, X, YouTube, Substack, LinkedIn, IMDB, others)
- Set up directory accounts or host account with trailer and description
- Write first 3–5 episode ideas and scripts
- Plan launch strategy (based on business plan)

- Once launched begin activating your 30 Day Social Media Plan (see example in this chapter)

Month 2 – Ready Episodes and Launch
- Record and edit first 3 episodes
- Design podcast cover art
- Record podcast intro, outro
- Submit podcast with placeholder to selected directories including trailer and description unless already completed and up
- Continue 30 Day Social Media Plan
- Update website with show news, including new episodes
- Capture screenshots/analytics of growth metrics
- Build email sign up form for free newsletter on website for episode updates

Month 3 – Growth of the Show
- Continue to publish episodes based on determined schedule
- Search for live events to network and share information on podcast, seek guests if desired
- Seek opportunities to speak and be a guest on other podcasts and other community events
- Ask friends, family and contacts to listen, rate, subscribe and give feedback
- Encourage reviews and ratings on platforms from strangers as appropriate
- Continue 30 Day Social Media Plan
- Continue to update website with show news, including new episodes
- Continue to capture screenshots/analytics of growth metrics and post exciting growth updates as desired

Month 4 – Next Phase of Content & Audience Growth
- Continue to publish episodes based on determined schedule
- Publish bonus episodes as desired (Bloopers? BTS teasers?)
- Use cache of episode highlights and quotes on social media in 30 Day Social Media Plan

- Engage with listeners (comments, DMs, funnels, emails)
- Collaborate and connect with strategic others
- Continue to update website with show news, including new episodes
- Continue to capture screenshots/analytics of growth metrics and post exciting growth updates as desired

Month 5 — Next Phase Marketing & Emails/Newsletter

- Send monthly newsletter featuring information on new episodes, bonus content, other content
- Offer exclusive behind-the-scenes or early access for subscribers and consider short-term promotional discount(s)
- Collect listener feedback for improving episodes
- Continue to encourage reviews and ratings on platforms from strangers as appropriate
- Continue 30 Day Social Media Plan
- Continue to update website with show news, including new episodes
- Continue to capture screenshots/analytics of growth metrics and post exciting growth updates as desired

Month 6 — Next Phase Marketing & Testimonials

- Share listener reviews, ratings, positive testimonials
- Feature guest highlights or success stories from episodes
- Track most popular episodes and content type and focus on more of same
- Continue to encourage reviews and ratings on platforms from strangers as appropriate
- Continue 30 Day Social Media Plan
- Continue to update website with show news, including new episodes
- Continue to capture screenshots/analytics of growth metrics and post exciting growth updates as desired
- Strategic review of first 6 months to determine what worked and what requires updating

Month 7 – Next Phase Marketing & Paid Advertising
- Run small ads to promote top episodes or guest interviews
- Target social media followers, lookalike audiences, and email subscribers
- Test and analyze alternative ad formats (video, carousel, story)
- Reward loyal listeners/seek new subscribers
- Continue to encourage reviews and ratings on platforms from strangers as appropriate
- Continue 30 Day Social Media Plan
- Continue to update website with show news, including new episodes
- Continue to capture screenshots/analytics of growth metrics and post exciting growth updates as desired

Month 8 – Continued Marketing & Content Expansion
- Record bonus episodes or mini-series
- Repurpose older episodes for new uses such as blogs
- Traditional marketing including networking events, trade shows, conventions, any related gatherings to niche area of podcast
- Try additional interactive content: polls, Q&A, or live streams
- Continue to encourage reviews and ratings on platforms from strangers as appropriate
- Continue 30 Day Social Media Plan
- Continue to update website with show news, including new episodes
- Continue to capture screenshots/analytics of growth metrics and post exciting growth updates as desired

Month 9 – Continued Marketing & Community Engagement
- Host a listener Q&A or live event podcast session
- Run additional contests or giveaways for listeners and loyal fans
- Highlight listener stories, questions, feedback in episodes
- Continue to encourage reviews and ratings on platforms from strangers as appropriate
- Continue 30 Day Social Media Plan
- Continue to update website with show news, including new epi-

sodes
- Continue to capture screenshots/analytics of growth metrics and post exciting growth updates as desired
- Consider additional revenue streams and purchasing additional promotional items that can be handed out to further spread the word about the show

Month 10 – Marketing Including Next Phase - Events
- In addition to regular monthly marketing activities and interactions plan a special event party, episode with after-party, live recording or other on-brand related event
- Promote event via email, newsletter, social media in addition to regular social media activities
- Collect sign-ups or registrations
- Share event recap as content
- Continue to encourage reviews and ratings on platforms from strangers as appropriate
- Continue 30 Day Social Media Plan
- Continue to update website with show news, including new episodes
- Continue to capture screenshots/analytics of growth metrics and post exciting growth updates as desired

Month 11 – Continued Marketing & Growth Push
- Run retargeting ads to website visitors and social media engagers
- Promote most popular episodes, guests
- Offer additional products/services such as limited-time content, courses, limited-edition merchandise
- Continue to encourage reviews and ratings on platforms from strangers as appropriate
- Continue 30 Day Social Media Plan
- Continue to update website with show news, including new episodes
- With updated analytics post teasers of year in review content and growth coming next month

Month 12 – Final Push with Year-End Review & Planning
- Share "Year in Review" episodes and other content along with regular 30 Day Social Media Plan
- Record a personal message and thank listeners while reminiscing about highlights/ top moments
- Review downloads, subscriber growth, and ad performance
- Plan next year's marketing/episode strategy

The above is just a sample and you want to tailor it to meet your specific needs. The general goal is to build awareness, engagement, listener and subscriber growth, audience size, and monetization however you have chosen to capture it. This calendar references a 30 Day Social Media Plan. Here is a sample of what that can look like.

30 Day Social Media Plan

In your 30 Day Social Media Plan you intend to:
- ✓ Teach people
- ✓ Share your story
- ✓ Show proof
- ✓ Be consistent

Create a chart to manage these tasks and repeat them monthly, updating it as required based on prior history of what worked and what did not. Include which social media platforms you want to be on with this activity.

WEEK 1 – Tell Your Story
Day 1: Tell who you are and what you do.
Day 2: Share how you started.
Day 3: Share one mistake you made and what you learned.
Day 4: Give 3 simple tips about your topic.
Day 5: Share a small win.
Day 6: Show behind the scenes (how you work).
Day 7: Ask your audience a question.

WEEK 2 – Teach Something

      Day 8: Share 5 easy tips.

      Day 9: Share one big lesson.

      Day 10: Make a short video teaching 1 thing.

      Day 11: Share a quote you like.

      Day 12: Share something you wish you knew earlier.

      Day 13: Share a success story (yours or someone else's).

      Day 14: Ask people what they want to learn.

WEEK 3 – Help People

      Day 15: Solve one common problem.

      Day 16: Share your daily routine.

      Day 17: Share tools you use.

      Day 18: Teach step-by-step how to do something simple.

      Day 19: Share your goals.

      Day 20: Share another tip.

      Day 21: Do a Q&A (answer questions).

WEEK 4 – Show Growth

      Day 22: Share what you improved this month.

      Day 23: Share a proud moment.

      Day 24: Share advice for beginners.

      Day 25: Explain how you make money (in simple words).

      Day 26: Share kind words someone said about you.

      Day 27: Share one strong opinion.

      Day 28: Share your future plans.

      Day 29: Invite people to follow or join something.

      Day 30: Look back and say what you learned this month.

Remember the best messages KISS (keep it simple sweetie) and for the best results you should be consistent, post every day, be honest and authentic and be helpful. You do not have to start your day 1 activities on calendar day 1 if today is the 23rd and you are ready to go. Start any day of the month you like and keep it going.

Much of what will go into this section in your business plan will be built out as you read the remaining chapters and decide what your podcast will be about, how you want to share it with the world, and how you will make money doing so.

Additional Appearances and Other Opportunities

Sometimes you get an opportunity to go beyond your business plan. When you do and you have time you should. The best way to grow your listening audience and make sales is to encounter actual humans. Press the flesh. Touch elbows. In-person networking is always going to be the fastest, most effective way to promote and sell your podcast to potential listeners and buyers of your merchandise and ads and whatever else you have for sale. For this reason consider in person, one-off opportunities that may come up at the last minute or are not on your calendar to get in front of people. Live networking beats just about everything else to truly reach and captivate another person with your message.

When you go to these events, it is rarely a good idea to be transactional immediately. But sometimes you can put up a sign and show what is for sale. Get a table at the local flea market and give out some bookmarks with a QR code to your website with details about your podcast show. Offer to be a keynote speaker for a local event that has some relevance to your topic. Volunteer to teach kids or young adults more on the topic your podcast covers if it is appropriate. Go into senior citizen homes and sing carols at the holidays or offer some other recreational event. These are the rich moments in life where you get to connect with the people who want your message and do not know it yet. This is how you scale to success. Money will come if the message is consistent, strong and resonates with others. You need to reach them to share the magic with them and that rarely comes from the comfort of your living room couch like your podcast itself does. So do not be afraid to go beyond the plan when you get these additional opportunities as you can fit them in.

All of these foundation pouring tasks take time and are worth it. You will get quicker and better at the activities that repeat once the one-time items are in place. It can be overwhelming at first, especially if your support team is small. Get your plans down and your business up quickly and then immediately focus your energy where it counts.

For my hit podcast The Naughty Librarian™ I had absolutely no plan in year one. I was winging it. With just word-of-mouth and no advertising spend it grew but this is not normal. It is better to have a plan.

Like anything else, what feels real and works for you might not work for someone else. You might have to make sacrifices and do less than you want to in the beginning in one or more areas just so you can get started. Social media marketing in particular takes a plethora of time and is a very thankless job at the start. Keep at it. You will find your tribe and they will find you. Your message will reach the world.

Financials

The "Financials" section includes your revenue model. It explains in more detail how you make money by giving away your free podcast to listen to as a driver of that revenue. It expands on information that was touched upon earlier and quantifies it in greater detail. It provides numbers, projections, and assumptions.

You can create a simple financial forecast based on expected revenue and costs if you want. Determine whether you want to ask Aunt Marge or Uncle Johnny for an advanced inheritance to help with some of the needed startup costs and funding to cover early operational needs.

I have always found some of this section fun and largely useless. Your financial projections are 'proforma' which means they are good guesses, assumptions, educated crystal ball musings. Oftentimes you do not really know who will buy or how much they will purchase before you start. Spend very little time on this section which is important and necessary primarily if a business wants to request funding from a bank or investor as it explains critical details those third-parties want to know. A podcast with no history in the entertainment industry started by someone who is unknown without collateral or connections is not going to be funded by a bank so this section can be microscopic to start.

The financial section of your business plan becomes more important once you have growth and want to take it to the next level in some way. Your history of sales and listeners make the projections more realistic. People may want to partner with you and invest in you once you have a track record of making money and you have what is called "proof of concept" in business.

Keep this section of your first business plan short for now as you start out since your time should be laser focused on getting your show out and getting to your first sale.

Appendices

In the "Appendices" section at the end of your business plan each Appendix appears that was too long to be put in the body of the plan. You can put any information referred to there and removed so it would not disrupt the flow of the contents. This can include resumes, research, spreadsheets, financial reports, detailed projections, and more.

Once each section of your business plan is complete, summarize and combine the information in your Executive Summary. Now it's time to implement your plan and start podcasting to the world!

CHAPTER 3
Finding Your Voice
Gear Up, Brand Up, Niche On, and Go!

This chapter covers four important areas of podcasting. They are: your choice of gear; your branding; your niche; and the basics to record your very first podcast episode so you can launch it into the world. If you have already started podcasting some of this might be a review. In order, here we go.

Gear Up!

Simple secret revealed: all you need in terms of gear to start a podcast is a microphone to talk into and an internet connection on your computer to capture the sound, make it something, and then launch that file as an episode strategically in the right places. This does not need to be a big and fancy process you need to hire a middle person or company for and you do not need to be a recording engineer either to be able to set up and use basic recording equipment to fully produce your podcast. You don't even need a really cool couch but it's the vibe for a lot of people so pick a color and some accent pillows, a stylish coffee table and some mugs and go for it, should you so desire.

This section introduces you to the basics of gear, the equipment you need to get started podcasting from your home. You do not need to overdo your setup. You just need to get these few elements right.

First, know that your podcast must be recorded with good, clear audio. People will stop tuning in if they have trouble hearing and understanding your episode because it is poorly recorded. You do not need to purchase expensive gear to get this clarity. Many popular podcasts have a simple setup. I did when I started. Sparse fully describes it: a laptop, a small external camera I attached directly to my computer through its USB port, a cloud-based video conferencing platform to record online meetings, and some editing software, and that was basically it. My expensive equipment did not get unpacked a lot of the time. The entire recording game has changed and in general quantity has become more important than quality (sadly) particularly for video but also for audio podcasts.

For the new podcaster this is great news! As you grow you can up your professional game and can get fancier if you choose, but to start, high-priced equipment is not required. It is a budget friendly side hustle to launch.

With your desktop or laptop accessing the internet and ready to go and any small external camera directly attached to it with a USB cable, you can select any cloud-based video conferencing platform to record your online meetings. Connection platforms like Zoom, Microsoft Teams, and others let you book and record online meetings. Once you have decided on one of these platforms and have started an account, learn how to use it. There are probably tutorials when you are logged in and there certainly are on YouTube. Search the current calendar year and the latest version of the platform and its app for a beginner's tutorial.

After completing the first meeting it gets easier. I promise. Ask a teenager if you're not sure how to set it up and record a meeting for the first go round. Do a test with someone as a mock interview to start, including where to save it and find it after so you know your entire production workflow in time for your first guest or show. You don't want to record a great interview and be unable to find it or use it for any reason.

You don't want to forget to turn the volume up to maximum on your computer so you hear nothing although it recorded sound. Make a checklist if you like so you don't miss any important steps.

You need a podcast microphone. There is one built into your computer. While professionals will say it is insufficient, it is sufficient. We used it for some episodes of the first two seasons. A decent podcast microphone that you can attach to improve the sound quality and enhance your audio clarity can be purchased for only a few hundred dollars. We do not endorse one product over another since there are so many great ones at affordable prices. This addition of an external microphone and its improved quality over the simple one built into your computer can make sound capture better with less background noise in your recording which means less post-production work on the backend of your project. Your time is valuable and limited when you are doing every task so make a decision that fits for you.

There are some basic differences in external microphones that will be introduced here so you are empowered in your purchasing should you choose to go shopping for a professional microphone. There are different types of microphones. The main two you want to know about are "Dynamic" mics and "Condenser" mics. Dynamic microphones tend to work best for broadcasting. They pick up lower frequencies and have reduced sensitivity. This means you'll have less background noise to remove later. They also work if you want to do lead vocals in a great touring rock band since they are durable on stage and give great performance even with all the bodily DNA flowing about and smacking into it (see the 'Rock Gods and Devils' episodes in Season 1 of the podcast The Naughty Librarian™ "TNL" for some amazing rock and roll stories for examples).

Condenser microphones have higher sensitivity and pick up a wider spectrum of frequencies. Sensitivity is useful for recording music but isn't ideal for spoken material. So unless you are cutting that album you are probably more interested in the other kind and not this one.

The ABC's of XLRs or USBs

Podcast mics have two types of interfaces: XLR or USB.
The XLR mics give you maximum versatility. There are a lot of

XLR mics to choose from, and they usually have a long durability. But XLR mics require an interface or mixer to hook into. You can run it through an interface if you record with multiple contributors. This can get costly for beginners.

USB microphones plug directly into your laptop. They are affordable, practical, and typically sound excellent. This mic is the best option for most podcast creators. You can build out setups for one-person, two-person, or three-to-four person podcast recording scenarios.

A lavalier mic can be used when recording a podcast episode in person with two or more people in a conversation. Each participant clips a small microphone to their clothing about 6–8 inches below the mouth, where a tiny capsule converts sound waves into electrical signals that travel by cable or wirelessly to a recorder or audio interface. Because the mic stays at a consistent distance from the speaker's mouth, it captures clear audio even as they move or turn their head. Each mic records to a separate channel, making it easy to balance voices during editing. Lavalier microphones can be used when recording into a video conferencing platform as well. Each person connects their wired mic through an audio interface or their wireless receiver into their computer as the selected microphone input.

That is it for basic gear to start. People will try to sell you on the idea that your set up has to have more to it but it does not. You do not even need headphones unless you want to really look the part and get into character with them sitting on your head ruining your hairdo. So you know, wearing headphones when recording can help you monitor and update the input–they do have that function. In simple terms they can let you hear your own voice and the other audio in real time so you can catch issues like volume, echo, or background noise while recording and make adjustments on the fly. You can also do this with just your ears if you have good listening skills and there is no extraneous noise in the room.

You also do not need a microphone flag unless you want one to take your brand visibility next level. A microphone flag is that cool square box around the mic with your logo. It is easy to make so do not order one unless you cannot even glue your fingers together in crafts class. To make a microphone flag if you want to, you cut out a small cube or triangular prism from sturdy cardboard or foam board, make a hole through the center just large enough for the microphone handle, assemble and glue or tape it together, then cover it with printed paper, vinyl, or stickers featuring your on-brand logo or design.

If you do want to build out a bigger set up this next short section of more advanced information is for you. If you do not, skip it if you like.

Attention audiophiles.

Recording a podcast remotely using advanced video conferencing software requires careful attention to signal integrity and system configuration. Start by ensuring each participant's audio interface is properly configured, with sample rates and bit depths standardized— preferably 48kHz/24-bit for podcast applications. Use a dedicated audio interface instead of onboard sound cards to minimize latency and jitter. You can possibly also encourage guests to monitor their input via headphones to prevent feedback loops, and enable high-fidelity audio or original sound settings in the application to bypass automatic compression, echo cancellation, and noise suppression algorithms that can compromise clarity.

To capture each participant cleanly, consider routing the audio through a multi-track recording setup, again only if you want to and have the patience to build out a set up. If you do, come over because I have an IKEA package here that needs some love and attention. Employ virtual audio drivers or digital audio routing software to split channels so each host and guest is recorded separately. This approach allows precise post-production control, including EQ, compression, and phase alignment. Make sure to test buffer sizes and CPU load beforehand, as real-time conferencing can introduce subtle dropouts or timing inconsistencies that may manifest in the final mix if unaddressed.

Network stability is a critical factor in maintaining clean recordings. If you are in a remote location or any of your guests are and the internet is spotty you might have to do more editing in post. A call could drop. It happens. Thankfully, not that often. The internet has come a long way for most of us. If they are agreeing to be a guest on your podcast they are probably technologically savvy enough to have reasonably decent working internet.

If a participant's connection fluctuates, recording locally with high-quality audio software and then syncing tracks in post-production if it is an option often yields superior fidelity compared to relying solely on the conferencing software's cloud recording. That works if they live nearby. It requires a safe space for everyone and sometimes guests who are strangers to the host are not comfortable going to another person's private residence even if your built out studio is totally lit. I've rented rooms in libraries before, which works great in these situations. Avoid hotel rooms like the days of old Hollywood press junkets. Same reason. The Weinstein days are over yet skunk spray lingers until the tomato juice moment. I'm a fan of supporting our local libraries and borrowing or renting the conference rooms they have. Ask what the formal process to do so is and any additional details you need to know and do like how long the rental is for and how much noise you can make. The Naughty Librarian™ recorded some episodes in libraries while on the road producing the show, with the help of some sweet, cardigan clad people to make it so.

For great audio you can actually record in a clothing closet or basement. It is comfortable, clean, silent, and makes a great sound studio because of all of those great wardrobe choices hanging about that dampens the sound waves causing a nice effect for your podcast sound. The downside is unless you are an expert in lighting you won't capture enough strong visuals to use for promo shorts to sell the show, and video is everything these days, especially when you want to make money with your show. Some basic back and side lighting is required if you want to record in this type of darker setting.

Now that you have your gear set up it is time to make decisions about what your brand is.

Brand Identity

Branding. Cattle ranchers do it to identify their walking steak so others can't claim it. What does it mean in the business world and for podcasting specifically? You and your podcast have a brand and are building it with every decision and episode you make. So this section will introduce you to what it is, how you should develop it and how to approach it when podcasting.

Branding is what people think and feel when they hear your podcast's name. It is not just your logo or cover art. It is your voice, your style, and the kind of stories or ideas you share. Your brand weaves through everything you do. Good branding helps listeners quickly understand what your podcast is about and why it is special. And it helps them remember you over every other podcast in the world. Use the same profile picture, colors, logo, art and message on all of your social media accounts, your website, and email updates as well as all of your podcast episodes to build and reinforce your brand. When your branding is clear, people remember you and can tell others about your show more easily.

For a podcaster, branding starts with knowing your main idea. You should be able to explain your podcast in one simple sentence. For us "The Naughty Librarian™ is a traveling podcast hosted by Alexander Loudon about storytellers and the stories they tell."

Ask yourself who you are in the world. Who do you want to be and how do you want others to see you? You are your show and all of your choices so it makes sense to decide and direct it. Specifically you want to determine what your podcast is actually making and saying in this world. What is the core of what you intend to do? What is your brand promise? What are you actually communicating, big picture with your show and its contents?

With the podcast The Naughty Librarian™ we used the word 'librarian' because we knew we wanted to talk to authors of books about their personal stories and the books they wrote. We used the word naughty because we took the position that we would talk to everyone, listen to everyone, and not be censored or silenced. People kept asking me "Are you The Naughty Librarian™?" so I realized "Yes, I am." For our branding, the title easily explained the subject. People needed it to be someone and so I became it for the show. The show became "TNL" for short.

Your podcast brand should clarify what customers can reliably expect from you and your creativity. If your brand promise is vague or unrealistic, the brand will struggle to stick in peoples' memories and they are unlikely to go back to it for future episodes and tell other people. Branding is defined largely by how customers interpret and remember their experiences with your podcast.

As you are coming up with ideas about your brand and what the title of your podcast could be that reflects that brand you might want to ask yourself some questions like "Does it signal my topic clearly including any expertise?" and "Does it help listeners quickly distinguish us from competitors?" If I had just called the TNL podcast "banned books" there would be no clear distinction between my podcast and dozens of others that essentially have variations on this name and are not uniquely identifiable as a result. It would not have clearly said what I was specifically doing which no one else was doing either.

Think also about any visuals you will add. Your podcast cover is a huge part of your brand. It is the first thing potential listeners see on podcast platforms and social media accounts and channels. It is a critical piece to get right. Your cover art should match the feeling of your show, such as fun, serious, or inspiring. Use the same colors, fonts, and style everywhere so people recognize your podcast right away. The name of your podcast should appear and it should be easy to say, easy to spell and easy to remember. Whatever you do, make sure your font is clear to read. If people can't read it, they can't remember it and will probably turn away when they otherwise might have listened and liked it. We chose a drawing that clearly projects our fun and lighthearted yet naughty theme and every time we use a font it is the same color scheme and it is always easy to read.

Think long term: if your business expands into other products or services, your podcast may become one item in a larger company portfolio under that brand umbrella and you want it to be fantastic!

Here are important details to consider when creating your podcast cover art.

Podcast Cover Art Technical & Design Guidelines

Attract Attention – Your cover art should stand out and pop. Design for scrolling behavior. The goal isn't to look good up close, but to stop someone mid-scroll. You can stand out and attract new listeners and fans by the instant opportunity to visually communicate the subject of the show with your podcast cover art.

Communicate Content – It should make the subject of your podcast clear at a glance. Potential listeners should know what your podcast is about just by observing your artwork. Too much symbolism or ambiguity can push people away. Personality and individual recognizability matter. Aim for artwork that represents you and your content accurately.

Keep It Simple (KISS Rule) – Keep It Simple Sweetie. Keeping it simple is your best option. Don't use too many words or fonts. Don't include more than four words on your cover art. Limit text to a maximum of 4 words and 2 font types. Make the title legible immediately. Large, thick text that can be read at a glance is more important than clever typography. Prioritize bold simplicity. One strong visual idea beats a busy design. High contrast, limited colors, and clean composition matter more than detail. Avoid clutter. Ensure it remains readable whether banner size or koozie size.

Avoid Equipment Images – Don't show mics, headphones, or podcast gear. Avoid extensive podcast imagery. Just as movie posters and streaming shows don't feature DVDs or TV sets, your podcast cover art shouldn't show podcasting gear. You don't need to remind people that they're tuning into a podcast. Seeing an actual podcast mic on podcast cover art has been overdone and looks amateurish now.

Use Faces Carefully – Use faces strategically. A clear, expressive face can increase attention and trust, but only if it's well-lit, close-up, and emotionally readable at small sizes.

Design for All Sizes & Platforms – Your artwork will be seen anywhere and everywhere there are podcast directories and libraries capturing it. You should also use it frequently in your promotional posts. Ensure readability at tiny icons (e.g., 55×55 px). Optimize for small screens first. The artwork should be instantly readable at thumbnail size, since most people see it on a phone before anywhere else. High contrast is critical because artwork is often displayed at 40–60 px tall in lists. You will use your artwork across multiple mediums and platforms, so it must appear good even at 55 × 55 pixels.

Stay Consistent – Match your overall branding and style. Brand consistency matters. Visual consistency over time helps recognition, even if individual designs aren't flashy. Consider documenting the details of your art files (such as fonts, sizes, and layout specifications) so the information can be accessed easily for new projects like generating merchandise without starting from scratch.

Research & Get Feedback – View the cover art of other podcasts to get ideas on what works and what does not in your opinion and why, and to get inspired. If needed, collaborate with a skilled designer to polish your final result.

Own Your Artwork – Use templates or experts, but maintain full ownership. Whether you do it yourself or get a friend or stranger to do your artwork, make sure you own it and have the right to use it or can afford to pay to use it if it is not yours. For more information on this see Chapter 4 Intellectual Property (IP). It gets expensive to have to pay someone else every time you drop an episode if all of the content is not yours to use free of charge, so if the cover art is yours to use you save a bundle right off the top.

Dimensions & Aspect Ratio – Square only (1:1 ratio) — anything rectangular risks cropping or rejection. The image must have a 1:1 aspect ratio (square) so it won't be distorted or rejected when the show is submitted. Minimum size: 1400 × 1400 pixels. Maximum size: 3000 × 3000 pixels. Designing at the maximum size (3000 × 3000 px) is recommended so it downscales cleanly everywhere.

Resolution & Color – 72 DPI is standard (higher DPI doesn't improve digital display). RGB color mode only — not CMYK.

File Format – JPEG or PNG only. These formats are widely supported across platforms and apps. PNG is often used when you need crisp text or graphics, while JPEG is useful when keeping file size small with photographic images. JPEG is usually preferred for smaller file sizes. If using PNG, avoid unnecessary transparency or effects that increase size.

File Size – Keep the file under ~500 KB to ensure fast loading and broad compatibility. Compression should not introduce visible artifacts, especially around text.

Text & Layout Safety – Keep all essential text well inside the margins (no edge-hugging titles). Assume automatic cropping may occur in some displays. Text should remain readable when the image is reduced to a small icon. Avoid fine lines, thin fonts, and low-contrast color combinations.

Content Restrictions (Technical, Not Creative) – No changing elements if the artwork is meant to be reused unless this is desired for strategy and branding. No URLs or platform badges.

Practical Design Check – Before finalizing, zoom out until the image is about the size of a phone app icon. If the title and main visual idea aren't instantly clear, it needs simplification.

Good podcast artwork suggests quality content. New listeners are more likely to tune to a podcast if they like its cover design. We at the podcast The Naughty Librarian™ love our podcast artwork and have even used artificial intelligence to get it to move. You want to love your artwork and feel like it truly represents what you are saying and doing with your podcast. Our artwork always appears in our podcast video intro and outro also, which will be explained next.

Branding Includes Sound

Your brand is also in your sound. Who does not love to hear classical radio host Terrance McKnight, actress Emma Stone or the actor Sylvester "Sly" Stallone speak because they have such unique and impressive voices? Your voice and tone also shape your brand. You cannot and should not want to change how your voice naturally sounds in your podcast unless you have some personal safety reason for doing so. It is you, after all. Keep it!

You can use your voice as a tool. This means being aware of and controlling how you talk, the words you use, and your energy level in your episode recordings. Try to sound the way you want to and the same to a degree in every episode so listeners know what to expect. If your show is calm, stay calm. If it is funny, keep it light and playful. Being consistent helps build trust with your audience. Of course, this is a rule that can be broken but if so it should be broken carefully and with intent.

You should record an audio "intro" and an "outro" for your podcast that is on-brand. It can be anything you want as long as it is short and clear. I recommend you include the podcast name and have some unique audio identifier such as a few beats or bars of some original sound. Start and end all of your episodes the same way, with this intro and outro sound that goes with your podcast cover art. This repetition helps your podcast look, sound, and feel familiar and professional to your audience. Listeners like knowing what is coming next. Like Pavlov's dogs in the famous psychology experiment who started salivating when they heard a neutral sound they became conditioned to, so will your listeners get ready for what is about to come after they hear and see that familiar introduction bit you repeat to start each of your podcast's episodes.

Talk to your audience in the same friendly way everywhere you show up. This makes your podcast feel like one strong, connected story. Do not worry if you have a small following where others have thousands or millions. Most people have just one or two social media platforms where they naturally grow their online voice and presence. We had over 100,000 podcast listeners in the first year and literally only 4 followers on the platform currently identifying as "X." Meanwhile on another platform where most of my tribe was, LinkedIn, thousands of the world's most powerful and influential people were following me, messaging with me and listening to my posts and podcast episodes. My podcast target market which consists largely of educated, intelligent, affluent and successful business people and world leaders heavily uses that professional platform so the connections came easily.

Over time, good branding helps your podcast grow. People begin to recognize your style and trust your message. They are more likely to subscribe, leave ratings and reviews, and tell friends. When you keep your branding clear and consistent, your podcast becomes easier to remember and harder to replace. Do not change it season over season because that will make it hard for people who are just discovering you in Season 3 to follow you — you follow? Besides, you want to spend your time doing more productive tasks that will grow your audience and your bank account. Set it and mostly forget it with a lot of your foundational items like cover art and audio introductory items. It is a requirement for global, long-term success.

Branding also shows up in your content choices. In addition to your niche (discussed next), your guests, if you select them, should be on-brand. Choose topics that match your main idea and avoid jumping all over the place. I was able to get a very famous person as a guest for my show early on and chose to turn it down because he had not written a book. Every other guest I had on was an author with a published book in the world. That was my niche. To not deliver this with a guest would have been confusing to listeners so I stuck to my formula and brand. I am not sorry I did. By not creating any confusion about what I was doing and what I was delivering with each season and episode my audience of listeners knew, and know, what to expect. It worked. The podcast grew globally and rapidly.

In podcasting, branding is how your show looks, sounds, and feels to listeners and done well it clearly, effortlessly describes your niche, which defines who your podcast is for and what specific value it delivers. This will be explained next.

Niche, Niche Baby

A niche in business is a clearly defined group of people with a specific problem, interest, or need that a product or brand is designed to serve. It is a tight lane where you focus on one specific type of person with one specific interest or problem. One example of a business niche is Starbucks which focuses on people who want premium coffee and a "third place" to hang out while they write their memoir or listen to their favorite Naughty Librarian podcast episode, not just anyone who drinks coffee.

To build a niche as a podcaster, you can work backward and begin with a topic, or you can define your target audience (the specific group of people you want to reach) and build it out from there. This requires identifying demographics (age, location, income) and psychographics (interests, values, habits) so your content speaks to a narrow, well-defined listener. At the same time, clarify your value proposition (the clear benefit listeners get from your podcast) so your show solves a specific problem or delivers a specific experience for that audience. Or just do what I did and decide what you like and consider how you want to start talking about it with other people. See if others are doing it. If not, you have a niche all to yourself (for now) and something great called "first mover advantage" which helps you grow and stay on top once you get there and other direct competitors launch podcasts with the same topic.

Next, establish content positioning (how your podcast is framed within the market). This means selecting a focused topic and a clear angle within that topic, rather than covering everything broadly. Use keyword research (the process of identifying commonly searched terms) to align episode titles, descriptions, and themes in the topic area. A consistent content strategy (a planned approach to what topics you cover and how often) reinforces your niche and makes your podcast immediately recognizable.

In podcasting specifically, a niche is the particular topic, audience, and problem your show focuses on. Think about the listeners. What would they want? To find your niche concentrate on a particular subject or category you are familiar with and can speak about. Ask yourself if others would like to listen to this topic and ask other people for feedback. Who would like and benefit from what you want to present? Rather than trying to appeal to everyone, a niche clearly defines who the podcast is for and what listeners will consistently gain from tuning in, such as education, entertainment, or inspiration around a particular interest. Ask yourself, what is the pixie dust that is going to propel the podcast show forward?

A strong niche combines three elements: a clear subject area (what you talk about), a defined audience (who you're talking to), and a distinct angle or perspective (how you're different). For example, instead of a general "business" podcast, a niche might be "marketing strategies for solo online coaches" or "startup lessons from failed founders" or "office bugs that bug and do not bug us" if you are going the etymological route. Having a well-defined niche helps your podcast stand out, attract loyal listeners, guide content decisions, and makes your show easier to discover and recommend. It is the heartbeat of your show.

Everyone can tell a story, even if it is not your experience you are talking about and you are only restating facts. With millions of weekly listeners and hundreds of episodes the current smash hit podcast "Crime Junkies" is one of the biggest true-crime podcasts in the world[1] yet they don't go creating victims by throwing them off bridges or into wood chipping machines. They have conversations and share facts. Their niche is scripted, story-driven true crime where a detailed case is narrated and discussed along with questions and commentary. They have an interesting niche people gravitate toward.

You need to decide what your niche is so you can create your podcast show and its episodes. Every podcast should have a secret sauce that makes their product or service something people will want that you provide and others do not. Your podcast is uniquely you, even if you cover a topic others are doing as well. You want to be original as much as possible and authentic to who you are and how you do it. This secret sauce in business is called a "unique selling proposition" (USP). For podcasts, there is no way of really knowing what people will like and listen to until you actually release and promote it. If you do something no one else is doing yet and it is interesting you may have an edge immediately. At the podcast The Naughty Librarian™ "TNL" I started doing something no one

---

1 Edison Research. (2025, February 5). The top 50 podcasts in the U.S. for Q4 2024 [Press release]. Edison Research. https://www.edisonresearch. com/wp-content/uploads/2025/02/Press-Release-The-Top-50-Podcasts-in-the-U.S.-for-Q4-2024.pdf

else was doing, although a lot of others were in the general space of books including recommending books and discussing banned books. There were a lot of people talking about what they liked and recommended in literature but no one was doing what I was. I was talking to the writers of books about their own personal stories and thoughts and their work. I talked with guests who were world famous with high accolades and others new to publishing that have not made their mark yet. Here is a screenshot I obtained when I tried to find other podcasts like mine early on, elucidating this point.

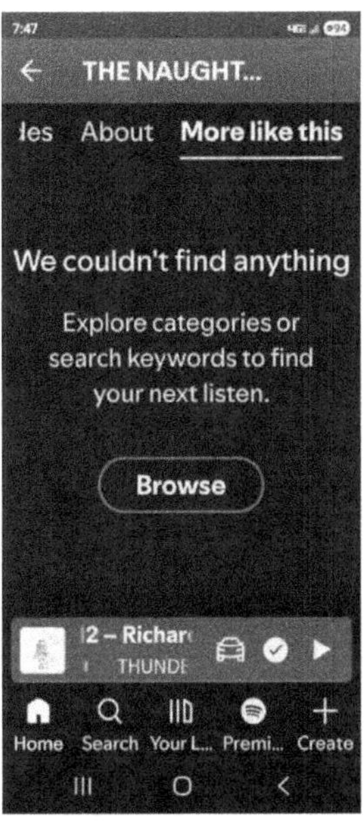

Your podcast can be about anything. Do not let anyone tell you otherwise. That said, if you have an eye on success you might want to find a niche area that is not being podcasted about well or even at all yet, as was our case. What are people interested in?

You want to execute your podcast niche flawlessly. This is not the same thing as saying you want it to be extremely polished. People like imperfections. You want to say something distinct in your podcast that makes people want to come back to listen to your show, something they cannot find anywhere else and want.

My podcast show description, honed for Season 3 when I figured out exactly what I was doing, really, and how explains my niche as follows:

The world's best storytellers and the stories they tell in intimate, personal conversations you won't find anywhere else with host Alexander Loudon. From Pulitzer Prize-winning authors to international bestselling authors and more, this is where the stories behind the stories finally get told! If you crave substance over shock and the best half hour of on-demand entertainment available anywhere, join listeners in over 150 cities and 23 countries and check out new episodes that drop every Wednesday, and become a Naughty Brat by following and connecting with us on our socials, joining our global community.

This describes my niche well.

Never mind the competition if there is something similar. Your formula could be better. That said, it is not a good strategy to aim to repeat what someone else is doing similar to the way they are doing it. It can potentially border on intellectual copyright infringement and it is just plain icky. Everyone loves competition as there is enough room for all but no one likes a thief or a copycat. Be an original. Approaching a subject others have talked about with a different slant is being unique. Technology exists to change the sound of a recorded voice easily and visually create an entire character. Maybe your niche involves this form of creativity?

The most important ingredient when deciding who you are as a podcaster and what your niche topic is concerns being authentic. Do that and others will feel it. They will appreciate it. If you keep this in mind, they should enjoy hearing what you have to present. What you do not want to do is to ask ChatGPT or some other platform or search engine 'how to be authentic' because the very act of doing so means you are not doing so and you are unlikely to find success. What you do want to do is go for coffee with yourself and have a great big think. Ask yourself what you like and what you know. Who are you really? What are your passions and interests? You collect beanies? Great! You yodel? Rock on! You're a cryovolcanologist ? An etymologist? Nice ice baby! Reach into your life and your work or side interests –these are goldmine places to draw your niche and unique content from. Figure out how to share stories about it and tell the world in your podcast.

Still no ideas? Start researching something brand new. Who do you want to be when you are not being you? Become that expert and build your voice, your set of rare and wonderful not-found-elsewhere stories.

Recording Your First Episode

Recording your very first episode can be a daunting task, but you've got this! The information in this section is here to help.

When in session recording the episode with the distinct and powerful 'Goddess of the Word' as I describe her, the Pulitzer Prize-winning poet Diane Seuss, she admitted candidly that she is not particularly good at oration, she is not much of a speaker. She likes to sit with words and choose them. She prefers to write them down. As a college professor she knew she used grammar wrong, sometimes out loud. She said she came to accept herself and realized it was "part of the package." So my advice to you on your first episode for your first show is to just do it. Do not strive for perfection. Be you and go for it. You will learn some tips along the way and improve in some areas and in other glorious ways you will stay imperfect and exactly you. You do not need schooling for this, you just need to start and try and keep on going. What made you stand out that you might have hated in grade school makes you stick out in a great way as an adult and makes people gravitate to you. How would our world look if Cindy Crawford had burned that mole? If Brooke Shields (who never ages…really!) had waxed those incredible eyebrows? If the amazing image architect Law Roach had changed his name? If Einstein cut his hair… Embrace yourself with confidence and know your uniqueness is fabulous.

Recording your episode so it is the best it can be does require a bit of preparation before you start talking. Here are some great tips, tricks and techniques to guide you if you are not sure how to make your first episode. Remember self love here and as long as you are making clear enough sound with great intentions, you have correctly clicked the recording button, and you have some editing software after to take out the unwanted bloopers, you will manage and thrive.

Decide on Your Seasons and Episodes

Determine how many episodes you want in each of your seasons and how many seasons you want to put out each year. Episode frequency must be consistent once you start.

Your podcast publishing schedule can vary based on how much time you have for your side hustle and how busy the rest of your life is. You might decide to publish daily, three times a week on the same days of the week, biweekly, monthly or on some other schedule. We recommend when you are in season to publish once a week to develop a rapport with listeners and create the habit of producing consistent material. That is what we did with the hit podcast The Naughty Librarian™ "TNL" and it worked. We also strongly encourage seasons and breaks so you don't reach burnout and to be clear on what these are so your fans know. Our listeners who enjoy the podcast The Naughty Librarian™ now expect two seasons a year with 14 episodes and some bonus content if we have more in the tank and want to. This also helps you and your fans de-grid. If it works, it will work and you determine the details. As long as you say what you do and you do it consistently, it will grow if it is good.

That said, absence only helps the heart grow fonder for so long so consider how long the breaks are carefully and accept the consequences. We at the hit podcast "The Naughty Librarian™ "TNL"" chose to have 14 episodes weekly in the spring and fall and then wrap, making the two seasons a year start around March and September each calendar year and giving a summer and end of year break respectively after each podcast season. We like four months off each year. We do not just sit by the pool working on our tans (well after the first few weeks). We use it to prepare for the next season to make it even better. This schedule takes a page from the playbook of the old days of television and many great, talented people approach streaming content this way. Others churn out content 24/7/365 to get a hit and then medically crash and have to take some time off. You don't get a badge for that. Time off helps. Remember this when you are planning and choosing how many seasons and episodes you will release. Your wellness matters and should always be a priority. If you can't show up, you can't show up to podcast (which is now a verb as well as a noun).

You can follow our pattern for seasons and episodes or select your own but whatever you do you must be consistent, communicate it and do what you say, otherwise you cannot effectively grow your audience or your side hustle podcast to make any serious money.

These are some of the most common publishing frequencies right now based on a random, nonscientific assessment. Publishing every 0—2 days (7%); 3—7 days (36%); 8—14 days (39%); 15—29 days (17%); and over 30 days (1%).

Now that you have decided how often you are releasing new episodes, you get to decide how long your episodes will be and what podcast format you will have.

Decide on Your Podcast Length

People are all over the map on podcast episode length, including within podcast shows. There is no one optimal podcast episode length but since people are busy and only have so much time I have repeatedly heard that anything over half an hour is work and less enjoyable for most people.

Make your episodes as long as they should be and no longer. Make all your episodes the same length whatever length you decide on. No one wants to work around you, but they will fit you in around their life when they can and know what to expect. Unless you are already famous you look like an amateur or ill-informed if your podcast episode lengths are erratic and different.

Some podcast episodes are less than five minutes each in length and others are much lengthier. Many shows have no length consistency from episode to episode. There are no standards that have emerged yet, no common episode durations for every podcast as there was for early television shows (which were 30 minutes or 60 minutes with room for commercials of about 8 minutes per every 30 minutes) and for early movies (which always were a standard 2 hours and it had better be a great movie like Titanic if it was 3 hours or more sitting in a theater eating overpriced, fake greasy popcorn while listening to an infant cry, seeing teenagers kiss and hearing that guy who talks through the movie…).

Podcasting is still unformed so even length of episodes for shows is fluid and changing rapidly. It is shocking how many podcasters do not set and stick to one time length. Because of this there are not clear statistics to compare podcast shows of different lengths. A rough approximation of podcast episode lengths based on loose averages (and this a non-scientific observation based on extensive independent review) is: length of podcast less than 10 minutes (14%); 10—20 minutes (15%); 20—40 minutes (31%); 40—60 minutes (22%); and, over 60 minutes (7%). Many successful shows hover around the 30 minute mark.

You can choose a format for your podcast. Your format should complement your podcast choice and feel sustainable. Ask yourself what energizes you. Do you love connecting with people or do you feel your best going alone? If you choose to have co-hosts, try to keep your group compact. Podcasting with more than two or four people makes scheduling a challenge and can make recording and editing more time consuming. Remember that some show formats require more post-production than others.

With The Naughty Librarian™ "TNL" my hybrid format is a storytelling, educational, unscripted and entertaining podcast, sometimes live and with guests in an informal interview that is more like a conversation. There can be sub themes and I occasionally have guest co-hosts.

Feeling like I am announcing the nominees at the Oscars, here is a list of some common podcast formats for you to consider, in no particular order.

1. Interview:

An interview podcast revolves around one host engaging with a guest in a structured or semi-structured conversation. The focus is on eliciting expertise, personal experiences, or unique perspectives from the guest. This format allows the host to act as a bridge between the guest's knowledge and the audience's curiosity. Preparation is key; good hosts research their guests thoroughly to craft insightful questions. Episodes can range from casual conversations to deeply analytical explorations, depending on the subject matter. The dynamic between host and guest shapes the tone and can make or break audience engagement. As mentioned, we have an interview format for the hit podcast The Naughty Librarian™ "TNL" and always have. People like to listen in on other peoples' conversations so this format always seems to work.

2. Solo (Monologue):

A solo podcast features a single host sharing ideas, reflections, or analyses directly with the listener. This format demands strong communication skills and the ability to maintain interest without external input.

Hosts can cover niche topics deeply, offering a personal lens or authoritative perspective. Episode structure often includes storytelling, commentary, or educational explanations. The host sets the pace, tone, and style, which means consistency is crucial to retain an audience. Preparation, scripting, and audience empathy are important to avoid monotony and ensure clarity.

3. Co-hosted (Conversational):

In co-hosted podcasts, two or more hosts engage in ongoing discussions on a topic. The charm comes from the chemistry between hosts, which can create humor, tension, or debate. Each host may bring complementary expertise or viewpoints, enriching the conversation. Episodes often feel spontaneous, though planning segments and topics enhances coherence. The format allows for more dynamic pacing, switching between storytelling, banter, and serious discussion. Balancing airtime and ensuring all voices are heard is important to maintain fairness and engagement. 4. Panel/Roundtable:

4. Panel Podcasts:

Panel podcasts feature multiple participants discussing a topic, typically moderated by one host. This format allows for diverse perspectives and often includes experts, enthusiasts, or stakeholders. Structure is essential to avoid chaos; moderators guide conversation, direct questions, and summarize key points. Panels can vary in tone from academic to casual, depending on the target audience. It encourages debate, contrast, and synthesis of ideas in real time. Audience engagement can be enhanced with Q&A segments or feedback integration, making listeners feel involved.

5. Narrative/Storytelling Non-Fiction:

Narrative podcasts are structured like audio documentaries or long-form stories based on real events or research. They rely on careful scripting, pacing, and sound design to immerse listeners. Hosts often combine narration, interviews, and archival audio to construct compelling narratives. The goal is to entertain while informing, creating an emotional connection to the material. Producing these podcasts requires research, storyboarding, and attention to audio quality. The format allows deep exploration of topics over multiple episodes or seasons.

6. Scripted Fiction/Audio Drama:

Scripted fiction podcasts are fully written audio productions with voice actors, sound effects, and music. They create immersive fictional worlds, often serialized over multiple episodes. Each character must have a distinct voice, and pacing is key to maintain tension and interest. Sound design and editing are essential to convey settings, action, and emotion. Writers must consider narrative arcs, character development, and cliffhangers to retain listeners. This format allows creative freedom but requires significant production effort and coordination.

7. Educational/Instructional:

Educational podcasts focus on teaching or explaining topics in depth, often with structured lessons or frameworks. The host assumes the role of instructor or guide, translating complex ideas into digestible content. These podcasts can cover academic subjects, practical skills, or professional development. They may include examples, case studies, or exercises for the audience to follow. Clear organization, pacing, and repetition of key points improve retention and comprehension. Interactive elements, like prompts or recommended readings, enhance learning outcomes.

8. News/Current Events Roundup:

News podcasts summarize and analyze recent events, trends, or developments in a given field. They provide context, interpretation, and expert commentary beyond what traditional news formats allow. Hosts must be well-informed and factually rigorous to maintain credibility. Episodes are often time-sensitive and may require frequent production updates. The format allows for concise daily updates or in-depth weekly analyses. Storytelling techniques and engaging delivery are crucial to differentiate from traditional news outlets.

9. Bite-Sized/Mini-Episode:

Short podcasts focus on delivering quick insights, updates, or tips in under 10–20 minutes. This format suits busy audiences seeking information efficiently. It requires concise scripting, clear messaging, and strong opening hooks to engage listeners immediately. Mini-episodes can supplement longer shows or function as standalone series. Frequency and consistency help build loyal audiences despite shorter duration. The format demands careful content curation to avoid oversimplification.

10. Repurposed Content:

Repurposed podcasts reformat existing material, such as lectures, speeches, webinars, or radio shows, into audio episodes. This approach maximizes content value without requiring full original production. Editing for clarity, pacing, and audio quality is critical to ensure the content feels like a cohesive podcast. Hosts may add commentary or context to adapt the content for listeners. The format is efficient but relies heavily on sourcing relevant, high-quality material. Repurposed content can reach new audiences or preserve archival knowledge.

11. Behind-the-Scenes/Process Breakdown:

These podcasts explore the creation, production, or workflow of a project, product, or event. The host takes listeners through each stage, highlighting challenges, decisions, and insights. This format is valuable for audiences interested in methodology, craftsmanship, or professional processes. Detailed narration and occasional interviews with participants enhance credibility. The format can combine storytelling with instructional elements to make processes engaging. Strong organization and pacing prevent episodes from becoming monotonous or overly technical.

12. Case Study/Interview + Analysis:

This format presents real-world examples or problems and deconstructs them through discussion or expert interviews. Hosts explain the context, outcomes, and lessons learned, providing a critical lens for listeners. The format encourages analytical thinking and application of concepts. Episodes often combine narrative, interview, and commentary elements. Preparation includes selecting relevant cases, identifying key insights, and scripting transitions. The structure balances storytelling with educational content.

13. Meditation/Mindfulness Guided:

Guided podcasts lead listeners through meditation, relaxation, or reflective exercises. Hosts provide verbal cues, pacing, and sometimes background music or ambient sound. The format emphasizes calmness, clarity, and mental focus, often incorporating breathing techniques or visualization. Episodes can vary in length from short exercises to full guided sessions. Consistency and tone are critical to establish trust and habitual listening. The format supports wellness, mental health, and mindfulness practices.

14. Game-Show / Quiz Format:

Game or quiz podcasts involve hosts or guests participating in competitions, trivia, or challenges. Episodes are structured around rules, scoring, and interactive elements that maintain engagement. The format can include humor, tension, and spontaneous reactions. Planning is required to design fair, interesting, and varied challenges. The format encourages audience participation through questions or contests. Editing ensures clarity and pacing for listeners.

15. Actual-Play / Role-Play:

Participants play games (often tabletop RPGs) or engage in role-playing scenarios recorded as the podcast. Episodes document game play, decisions, and character development in real time. Storytelling, strategy, and improvisation are key to creating entertaining content. Editing balances length, pacing, and clarity for the audience. Hosts may explain rules or background to make episodes accessible to newcomers. This format blends narrative, collaboration, and entertainment.

16. Hybrid/Mixed Format:

Hybrid podcasts combine elements from multiple formats, such as interviews, storytelling, solo commentary, or panel discussion. This flexibility allows creators to experiment with pacing, tone, and content delivery. Episodes can cater to different listener preferences within one show. Structuring hybrid episodes requires careful planning to avoid confusion or overcomplexity. Creativity is rewarded, but consistency is still important for audience retention. The format can evolve over time to reflect audience feedback.

17. Storytelling Fiction Anthology:

Each episode presents a standalone fictional story with unique characters and settings. Unlike serialized dramas, episodes can be consumed in any order. Writers focus on plot, character arcs, and concise storytelling. Sound design, music, and voice acting enhance immersion. The format allows exploration of different genres, themes, and styles. Anthology podcasts are ideal for creative experimentation and diverse narrative approaches.

18. Listener Q&A / Ask-Me-Anything:

Episodes are driven by questions submitted by listeners, which the host answers thoughtfully. This format fosters direct engagement and community building. Hosts must balance spontaneity with preparation to provide valuable responses. Episodes can include commentary, analysis, or storytelling alongside answers. Structuring responses clearly ensures accessibility and maintains flow. This format can sustain long-term engagement by responding to evolving audience interests.

19. Live/On-Location Recording:

Podcasts recorded live or on-location capture interactions, ambient sounds, and real-time reactions. This format creates immediacy and authenticity for listeners. Hosts must adapt to unpredictable environments while maintaining clarity and pacing. Editing may include crowd noise management and post-production polishing. The format is ideal for events, fieldwork, or experiential storytelling. It emphasizes presence and engagement that studio recording cannot replicate.

20. Seasonal/Themed Series Format:

A multi-episode limited series is centered on a cohesive theme, story, or topic. Episodes are planned with a narrative or conceptual arc. This format encourages deep exploration over a structured period, creating anticipation for listeners. Hosts must maintain consistency in tone, style, and pacing. It allows experimentation with storytelling and production techniques within a contained framework. Seasonal formats can attract both episodic listeners and new audiences with focused, high-quality content.

21. Educational Podcast:

An educational podcast is designed to inform and teach the audience about a specific topic, skill, or area of knowledge. The host typically presents content in a structured, clear, and engaging way, often breaking complex concepts into digestible segments. Research and accuracy are critical, as credibility builds trust with listeners who seek to learn something valuable. Episodes may include explanations, step-by-step guides, case studies, or curated examples to illustrate key points. Some educational podcasts incorporate occasional guest experts or interviews to deepen understanding, while others rely solely on the host's expertise. Consistency in format and pacing helps maintain listener engagement and ensures that each episode delivers tangible learning outcomes. For example, an educational podcast with a focus on biology subjects could dive into "Gut Bugs and Glory," uncovering the quirky and surprising ways our microbiome runs the show behind the scenes.

We at the podcast The Naughty Librarian™ "TNL," by interviewing the most successful and prominent people in the literary world including bestselling authors and Pulitzer Prize-winning authors, are also making history doing educational content. Hybrid! I was so moved when I interviewed poet extraordinaire and recluse Dianne Seuss with co-host the equally talented Gail Wronsky who happened to be her close friend of decades. I realized I captured a moment history will look back upon and appreciate. It was such a powerful moment of success for me extending way beyond ad sales, good reviews and other appreciation from the world. I was able to give this to the world and its present and future beings. I had the opportunity to do that with my hybrid podcast format. It was so special.

Decide if You Will Have Guests

Based on your brand, niche and format you may or may not have guests come on your podcast show. Guests are the best, and the worst, but mostly the best. I've chosen to interview authors who are convicted criminals, Pulitzer Prize-winning authors and everyone in between. I've created a safe space for my guests and sometimes it has gone pretty wild. Do not count out guests who might not be your cup of tea because they might be for someone else. Also, local neighborhood heroes can be as fantastic as the more famous ones, especially if they are rock stars in your chosen niche.

Guests like getting the spotlight. Why shouldn't they? So many platforms discourage self promotion. Your podcast helps their voice reach others. It is truly a win-win-win . As you get content, they get to expand their message to reach your listeners. Listeners will be entertained and possibly informed.

A note on protecting yourself when seeking and booking guests. Do not give any identifiable information when communicating with strangers beyond providing your name and your LinkedIn professional profile or something similar, even if they seem to be legitimate. Get a burner cell phone number with voicemail or a switchboard . Use a post office PO Box address or other professional address that is not your home if you do not have an office or business address. This is for your safety. It prevents fraud and other crimes from being committed against you. I have personally encountered entire fake websites with false agent contact information and false information about conferences and seminars claiming to sell tickets. There are some lousy people in the world who just want to cause you trouble. Do not let them.

Do not pay for guests unless you know you are dealing with the professionals who actually represent them. It is rare to need to pay for a guest at all unless you are a traditional Hollywood or New Hollywood streaming show. When someone asks for payment it is usually a red flag, a warning that they may not be legitimate. Other red flags include unprofessional emails like gmail or hotmail instead of a business one (although I sometimes use my personal email and many of my guests do as well), unusual website addresses, and relatively low appearance fees for major A-List celebrities. Someone built out an entire website claiming to represent author and actor Keanu Reeves and when contacted said yes to us. They requested a very low appearance fee and our team found it to be fraudulent after engaging in the appropriate due diligence. A follow up call to his talent agency revealed it was a scam. Our team was not out any money since we confirmed the offer was fake before booking. We knew

Keanu was worth much more than the requested amount! We also know from his agency that a lot of other people were not as lucky and have paid false fees to book him (or so they thought).

> *Dear Keanu· We still want you· Your books are great· Please reach out through your people if you are feeling it back and we will make it happen! For everyone who has been duped trying to shoot their shot to book you! The Naughty Librarian™ host Alex*

Most people are good but some have not discovered the love path is the best one. Basic awareness and precautions are required, fellow podcasters.

Write a Podcast Outline

Rambling is one of the most frequent mistakes new podcasters make. The best method to combat this tendency is by creating a podcast plan or outline. Even taking a few moments to jot down a series of bullet point form ideas will dramatically enhance the flow of your recording session. If you're working with a co-host, share the outline with them so you can collaborate on it. For me, to start the podcast The Naughty Librarian™ "TNL" I had a working template with three sections. I structured it as follows.

Part 1 of the template included saying hello and thank you to everyone involved. It introduced the audience to what was about to go on, provided the name of the guest and some descriptive details about that guest including what publication(s) they had out and any awards and recognition received. It included introducing and thanking a co-host if I had one (and, so far, I like to slot one in each season to give it flavor and another layer).

Part 2 was the body of the recording session where I asked my guest questions from my research. Yes, I do extensive research for each guest. If you think you do not need preparation and research, enjoy the episode of the Sex and the City reboot "And Just Like That" where Carrie Bradshaw (the amazing SJP irl) is saved by her computer from a useless, externally beautiful podcaster. Do your homework so you do not embarrass yourself and waste everybody's time. Or risk the wrath of a protective computer!

Part 3 in my template concluded with pleasantries and making sure I gave the guest an opportunity to pitch whatever they wanted to. Many creative people who will be on your podcast have one or more projects they want others to know about, and if you are getting their time free for your content it is nice to give them the spotlight to shamelessly self promote. We are all in this together. You can edit out anything that is too commercial for what you are doing and how if you must. I edit out most specific businesses that are mentioned because I have companies that pay me to advertise and it is not fair to them otherwise. I'll give away freebies when groceries and heating bills are free. Other than that, this is their spotlight time to shine and they can take it anywhere. I end it by thanking everyone and reminding the listeners about the podcast they are listening to.

Whatever you do with your outline, do not over do it. It will sound stiff if you do. Less is more. I recommend having an outline in bullet point form and only as detailed as you need with questions or information from your research and then getting on that horse and letting her run! With no room for discovery and letting the unexpected happen a lot of the sparking moments that could occur will not be allowed to bubble up. Those sell the show and are the reason we all do this. Nothing like live!

Pick a Good Place and Time to Record and Have Proper Technique

Whenever possible, record in a quiet environment with plenty of furniture, curtains, rugs, or carpeting. It feels cozier and it helps the sound. Set up your gear and have your equipment tested and ready. Have extra charged batteries on hand. Have any online platforms you are using logged into and open, ready for the other participants if there are any. Be at least 15 minutes early to accommodate any unforeseen technology issues or other problems.

If you set a live or online meeting with a guest be sure to send them information days or even weeks before the meeting so they can put it in their calendar and join at the correct date and time. If you are like me and are always traveling and interviewing people across the globe, factor in time changes using and sharing the Coordinated Universal Time (UTC) time zone information. Also do not forget Daylight Saving Time (DST) which is the practice of only some of us on the planet adjusting clocks an hour earlier or later twice a year. Also, if your guest travels too make sure you ask what time zone they are in on the date you have both selected. It is a weird reality, scheduling and booking globally with multiple time zones and clock changes but is easily manageable as long as you remember and attend to all of the variables. If something goes wrong with the schedule, keep calm and podcast on. Apologize and fix it as needed. Accept other people's best on the other side of this and all that is meant to be will be. It has been my experience that sometimes older guests or those who are frail for any reason benefit from extra reminders.

Remember that good audio is important, and everyone needs to be clear and loud enough to be heard, including you, so if you are just using your desktop or laptop computer you need to stay consistently close to your computer microphone when you record without looking strained or weird. Do not make nervous noises or drum your fingers and learn to stay still while looking relaxed. You can support your guest by suggesting they lean closer if the sound you are hearing from them while recording is too soft. They appreciate you being in their corner for their success.

If the audio is not perfect from your recording, but it is a great show, don't be afraid to use it anyway while you are learning by experience and tweaking your set up to make it better. It's surprising how much an audience will put up with, for a short time at least, when the content is captivating. For the hit podcast The Naughty Librarian™ "TNL" the very first episode was shot live on location at a resort with a pool, restaurants and a noisy tiki bar. We had great fun and captured absolutely horrible audio, despite multiple cameras, and much was learned. We heard the dog panting, his leash jingling, and more. For this episode and most others we kept it clean in post-production and did not add any effects either or take out the dog noises. To be honest we are not sure how anyone even liked the first episode. It was so rough (ruff?). The audio was bad and the guest author was panting and farting through most of it . But it was also awesome content because it was so raw, honest, comedic and so much fun for everyone involved. Every time I hear it, I laugh out loud. To this day it remains one of our most popular episodes. Go figure. People like true stories and panting and farting dogs as well as Pulitzer Prize-winning poets sharing eloquently. The moral to that furry story is that if you are doing your own original great work, just do your best and throw it out there. It will probably work.

If you do use an external microphone that you are adding to your computer or otherwise speaking into, position your mouth 2" to 4" away from the mic for the cleanest output. The optimal distance may differ slightly depending on your device so read up on it beforehand.

If you notice too many plosives or harsh sibilance in your tracks, the simplest fix is to move off-axis from the microphone. Set your mic to the side, angled slightly toward your voice. This adjustment prevents bursts of air from striking the capsule and produces more natural audio.

Record a Test Track

Try recording yourself speaking at a consistent level in several different positions. Then, review the recording to determine which placement provided the best audio and also video results. Don't stress about mistakes, stammers, or pauses. Noise reflects off hard, flat surfaces, so minimize these whenever possible. You can also treat your space with foam panels mounted on the walls to improve acoustic clarity.

Here are some additional professional tips you can follow to get a good microphone and recording technique for your first episode. Some will be familiar information and some will be new.

• Use a pop filter or windscreen to reduce plosives and protect the microphone from harsh bursts of air.

• Do not eat or drink while recording. No one wants to hear you slurp or gulp, really. Gross.

• Speak as clearly and loudly as you can while remaining natural. Slowing it down so it feels too slow is a good way to have it not be too slow. Try test samples with mock interviews with a friend to compare your speaking speeds and how they actually sound when you are hearing them back. This is how you find your voice speed if you are new to it. Aim to avoid using the word "like' for every third word, and if you do not speak well join a local group of debaters or speakers to get better at it. No one will listen if no one can understand what is being said.

• Record separate tracks for each participant whenever possible if this is how you choose to set up your studio, even in remote setups, to allow precise editing in post-production.

• Monitor levels in real time using headphones to catch clipping, background noise, or uneven volume before recording gets too long. If you do not want to wear them another crew member can do so if you have one.

• Create a "room tone" track of silence for 30–60 seconds to fill gaps and make edits sound seamless.

• Label and organize your files immediately after recording and add numbers and speaker names to save time in post-production. Upload them safely to the cloud to reduce single device storage risk.

• Do a short test recording before the main session to adjust microphone placement, gain, and acoustics, especially when recording in new environments.

Finally, a brief word on controlling nervousness before recording a podcast, especially if it is live. Controlling nerves before a live podcast begins with preparation. Familiarity with your episode structure, having a clear outline and knowing your equipment is ready can significantly reduce anxiety. When you do your preparation and research and feel confident in your material and questions if you have guests, and if you know the flow of topics, key questions, and transitions, or whatever else you choose to have on your show, your mind can focus on delivery rather than improvisation. Reviewing notes or practicing your opening lines aloud beforehand also helps your voice and timing feel more confident.

Physical preparation can also make a big difference. Simple breathing exercises—such as deep diaphragmatic breaths—help lower heart rate and release tension. Gentle stretches or rolling the shoulders and neck can reduce physical stiffness that often accompanies nerves. Hydrating beforehand and having water or herbal tea with honey nearby ensures your voice remains strong, smooth and consistent throughout the recording. Do not drink or eat too much before recording to avoid needing a bathroom break.

Mental framing and mental toughness is equally important. Remind yourself that minor mistakes are natural and can be edited later, so the pressure to be perfect is unnecessary. Visualizing a successful recording session or thinking of your audience as a small group of friends rather than an unknown mass can also calm anxiety. Some hosts use positive affirmations or mental cues to reset focus between segments.

Doing a short test or warm-up segment before going live is good for your nerves and checking the equipment. Speaking into the microphone for a minute or two, testing sound levels, and familiarizing yourself with the recording environment just before starting the recording helps shift your focus from nervous anticipation to active participation. The combination of preparation, physical readiness, and mental reframing allows you to approach a podcast recording session with confidence and clarity. Since I have already completed a few seasons and several dozen episodes as The Naughty Librarian™ I do not get nervous before shooting anymore. I relish the chance to meet a new person and learn their stories. That said, if I can finally figure out how to get Mr. Reeves, Mr. Stephen King or Ms. Joanne K. Rowling on the show, I'm sure I will want to employ some meditation and leave out the coffee beforehand.

Now that you have made all of your important decisions and have done all of your preparation to know what you need to capture in this first episode it is time for lights, camera, action! You are in production, on the set. Remember to click or hit the record button and just relax and do your best.

Once this first recording is successfully 'in the can' the work begins (sorry). Later chapters teach you the work that comes next so you can finish preparing it and launch your wonderful new show out to the world.

So you know as you sit in your cube farm or on the bus reading this and imagining your success once your new hit podcast goes live, Steve Carell became widely known in part due to a small mistake during his audition for The Office. In one scene, he accidentally flubbed a line and improvised a goofy, awkward pause. Instead of hurting his chances, the casting team loved the unpolished, human quality it added to his character, Michael Scott. That mistake helped define the awkward, endearing persona that became iconic, launching him to household-name fame. It's a great example of a small error that turned into a career-defining moment.

Do your best for your first episode and every one thereafter. Accept that bloopers and mistakes are a part of life, and the flavor of life. It just might be what makes you the world's next big influencer!

CHAPTER 4
Speak Softly and Carry
a Big IP Lawyer!
Your Entourage

Ask a lawyer. This chapter provides free legal information to help you in the podcasting business. Legal issues matter. How you set up your business podcast helps you make money and how you are aware of the law when making and growing it helps you keep it, or not.

In this chapter we clearly teach you the introductory legal workings and mechanisms involved in the business of podcasting. Podcasting in the entertainment industry is a grab for the attention of audiences consuming Intellectual Properly (IP). The friendly battle of rivals in podcasting with multibillion dollars to be earned is like King Kong vs Godzilla vs Mothra in a china shop. You need to show up with something to survive, thrive, fight to grow, and stay alive. Kong has raw, overwhelming strength. Godzilla has atomic breath. Mothra has divine resilience. Your

Kaiju power is legal knowledge and here it is.

For this chapter we reached out to an expert in the field, Mr. Ruben DeLeon, owner of DeLeon Law Group P.C. Mr. DeLeon is an educated, experienced legal expert in Intellectual Property transactions and litigation. Our digital conversation touched on the major questions people have about the law and the craft and business of podcasting. Here is the most important legal information you need to know for your Side Hustle Podcasting business.

Host Alex: Hi Mr. DeLeon, thanks so much for contributing your time and expertise to this chapter. It is greatly appreciated.

Mr. DeLeon: Hi Alex, my pleasure.

Host Alex: What is Intellectual Property?

Mr. DeLeon: Intellectual Property (IP) refers to legally protected rights in creations of the mind — things you create rather than things you physically manufacture. For a podcast, IP typically includes:

- The podcast name
- The logo and artwork
- The audio recordings
- The intro music
- The episode scripts or outlines
- The website and written content
- The video versions or clips
- The brand reputation and goodwill
- Any course, book, or paid subscriber content built from it

A podcast is not "just audio." It is a bundle of intellectual property rights.

Host Alex: What IP is associated with a podcast? What are copyrights, patents and trademarks as they relate to my podcast and how can I protect them in setting up and operating my show?

Mr. DeLeon: Here is how the three core IP categories apply:

Copyright (Automatic Protection)

Copyright protects original creative expression fixed in a tangible medium. For your podcast, copyright covers:

- Audio recordings (each episode)
- Video recordings

- Show notes and scripts
- Website text
- Cover art
- Intro/outro music (if original or licensed)
- Subscriber-only video content
- Social media captions (if original enough)

Protection begins automatically upon creation, but registration with the U.S. Copyright Office gives you: the ability to sue in federal court; statutory damages; and, attorney's fees (if timely filed). For weekly episodes, many podcasters register in batches.

Trademark (Brand Protection)

Trademark protects names, slogans, and brand identifiers that identify the source of goods/services. For a podcast, trademarks protect:
- Podcast name
- Logo
- Tagline
- Possibly recurring segment names

You protect this by:
1. Clearing the name before launch
2. Filing a federal trademark application (Class 41 – entertainment services)
3. Using ™ (before registration) and ® (after registration)

This is critical if you plan:
$ Sponsorship deals
$ Merchandising
$ Licensing
$ Live shows

Patent (Usually Less Relevant — But Not Always)

Patents protect new inventions or processes. Most podcasts do not involve patentable subject matter: however, patents could apply if you create:
- A novel podcast distribution platform
- A unique recording technology
- AI-driven audio processing systems

Your show content itself is not patentable.

Host Alex: How do I protect my website, subscriber content & clips?

Mr. DeLeon: Each component has its own protection layer. Website content can be protected through copyright by registering major works. A website name may be protected with a trademark obtained through federal registration. Paid subscriber videos should be safeguarded using both copyright and contracts, typically through clear Terms of Service. Social media clips are protected by copyright and enforced using platform enforcement tools. Finally, an email list can be protected as a trade secret through strong privacy policies and security measures.

Important tools:

- Terms of Service
- Privacy Policy
- Guest release agreements
- Contributor agreements
- Platform takedown (DMCA notices)

Behind-the-scenes content is fully protectable if original.

Host Alex: How do I protect my weekly audio episodes?

Mr. DeLeon: Each episode is:

1. A sound recording
2. A literary work (script or structured discussion)
3. Possibly a derivative work (if you use third-party material)

Best practices:

▷ Use written guest releases.

▷ Register episodes (individually or in batches).

▷ Maintain production files as proof of authorship.

▷ Use watermarking or audio fingerprint services if concerned about piracy.

Host Alex: What can't be protected?

Mr. DeLeon: Certain things are not protectable:

- Ideas (only expression of ideas)
- Facts
- Titles alone (short phrases not used as brands)
- General formats (e.g., "two people interview guests weekly")
- Public domain content

You cannot protect:

- The concept of having interviews

- The idea of discussing poetry or politics
- General conversational style

You protect your specific expression — not the concept.

Host Alex: Free speech—are there limits? Can I and my guests on the podcast say anything we want?

Mr. DeLeon: You and your guests do not have unlimited freedom. Limits include:

1. Defamation (false statements harming reputation)
2. Copyright infringement
3. Invasion of privacy
4. Right of publicity violations
5. False advertising
6. Incitement or criminal conduct

Free speech protects against government censorship — not civil liability.

A podcast host can be liable for guest statements if:

- They knew it was false
- They acted with reckless disregard
- They materially contributed to defamatory content

Host Alex: What if someone uses my podcast name later?

Mr. DeLeon: If you started first:

If you have no trademark registration you may have common law rights (geographic scope) and you must prove priority. If you have federal registration you can: send a cease and desist; file a USPTO opposition; and, bring federal infringement action. Early registration is significantly stronger.

Host Alex: Is there any free content I can legally use?

Mr. DeLeon: Yes:

Public Domain

- Works published before 1929 (in U.S. as of 2026)
- Government works (U.S. federal)
- Expired copyrights

Creative Commons

- Must follow license terms
- Some require attribution

- Some prohibit commercial use
  Always confirm:
- License type
- Whether derivatives are allowed

Host Alex: Can I use audio from a pop star or actor? What if I use some audio from a singer or actor in my podcast episode either directly or remixed in some way?

Mr. DeLeon: Using commercial music or audio clips usually requires:

1. Master recording license
2. Musical composition license
3. Possibly sync license (if video)

Fair use may apply in limited circumstances:

- Commentary
- Criticism
- Parody
- News reporting

But entertainment use, introductory music and background clips are rarely fair use. Remixing does not eliminate infringement.

Host Alex: AI and podcasting. What role does artificial intelligence (AI) play in my podcast from a legal perspective if I use it to generate some of my content or ads or related derivatives from it?

Mr. DeLeon: If you use AI potential issues include:

- Who owns AI-generated content?
- Is the output infringing?
- Are training data issues implicated?
- Disclosure obligations in advertising?
  Key legal themes:
- Human authorship requirement for copyright
- Contract terms with AI providers
- Deepfake / voice cloning liability
- Disclosure requirements for AI-generated ads

If AI creates content with minimal human input, copyright protection may be limited.

Host Alex: How is IP different internationally?

Mr. DeLeon: The core themes of copyright, trademark and patent are global. Registration systems differ. Moral rights are stronger in Europe. Enforcement varies. Fair use differs (U.S. is broader) A U.S. trademark does not automatically protect you in Europe. Podcasting is global distribution — IP protection is territorial.

Host Alex: Once again thanks Mr. DeLeon.

CHAPTER 5
It's About the Money, Honey
So Grow Your Wealth, Stealth

This might be the most important chapter you will read if you want to make money podcasting. The podcasting business is a business. If you are in it just to have fun and hang with a friend in a cool, large sweater clutching a big stylish coffee mug and lazing about on a cozy modern couch dishing about whatever just happened on the news or in Hollywood then go ahead and have as much fun as possible. If, however, you are reading this book to learn how people earn income doing the exact thing because you want to as well, then the information in this chapter is critical to your success. It explains the subtle, important differences in how you set up and operate from the start to monetize your podcast.

You can't un-launch digital content once it is out in the world and get a redo on it, especially once you have a following. You cannot ask for another growth wave of views or followers because you were not ready.

There is a way you should structure every element of your podcast from the start so you are in control of all of the pieces and can manipulate them in your favor financially, especially when it takes off. You need to be a bit stealth with some of these activities. What you are doing looks the same as what everyone else who is podcasting is doing, but it is not.

About a billion people watch podcasts on YouTube monthly.[1] A handful of top creators who upload their podcasts to YouTube receive sizable payouts while many and most podcasters who upload all of their podcast episodes receive absolutely nothing. We at The Naughty Librarian have never put our full podcast episodes on YouTube and have yet to put more than the occasional short video trailer or promotional short video there. YouTube is important, and you can use it from the start, and should use it for promotion in your 12 Month Marketing and Social Media Plan developed in Chapter 2, but you do not want to hand them all of your content free while they make billions on it and give you nothing in return. That is not even a hobby. That is volunteering.

If you give away milk, nobody has to buy a cow. Everyone out there who is telling you how to launch and promote your podcast is explaining to you how to give away your cow. This includes major and smaller platforms, directories, powerful influencers who are paid to say that, and more. I simply cannot believe how many people are giving away their cows and how few people are able to see the obvious–that content is the gold in this gold rush. You can sell it instead of just giving it all away. You can only do so though if you have this attitude and direction from the start.

In this era of podcasting you don't just have a video strategy, video is your strategy. Everything is video today. So you record your podcast in video and upload the actual podcast episodes as audio only with an on-brand placeholder as the visual through the entire episode. It can show the cover art, the title, the season number and episode number, and a total chronological episode number (TCEN) if you like, and that is it. Avoid putting much more than that on your placeholder as it will only be seen as a small icon in most places. You can search our podcast and its episodes

<hr>

1   Carman, A. (2025, February 26). A billion people are watching podcasts on YouTube every month. Bloomberg. https://www.bloomberg.com/news/articles/2025-02-26/a-billion-people-are-watching-podcasts-on-youtube-every-month

to see how we do this (thanks for leaving a 5-star rating after listening to a bit of it while you are there, should you be so inclined).

The subtle difference between doing it this way and what most other people are doing is that you are actually uploading your episode everywhere as a video file, an mp4 file, not an audio one, although it is really just audio you are releasing. So the platforms take your podcast and push it in their feeds like it is video, since video is prioritized. This along with strategic keywords in your episode descriptions and titles, Podcast Search Engine Optimization called Podcast Search Optimization (PSO) in your copy, and strong cover art and thumbnails (detailed elsewhere in this book) for the eye candy to draw more listeners everywhere they do see that placeholder, and the algorithms and eyeballs will love your podcast episodes. Your audience will organically grow, like ours did.

When you have your video (but actually audio only) podcast with one or more episodes ready to unleash to the world, you currently get it out on a few major platforms and some smaller ones to reach the world (see the chapter on distribution). This is a fast-changing landscape with a few major behemoth players right now. Should the names of these major suppliers change it is just a game of thrones, and a lot of the general content that appears here will stay similar.

So now you probably realize that by recording your show as video and uploading your podcast everywhere as a video with just audio with placeholders you have full control of all of the video you record. You can break the best parts into short segments and use them in your social media strategy. You can use some of it as behind-the-scenes content to sell if that is part of your revenue strategy. You can do anything you want with it. You are in full control of your content now.

Everyone wants to see your video. Especially if you refer to it in the podcast show dialogue (e.g. "wow, you have to see this, it's hard to explain"). If people didn't listen with their eyes there would not have been 16 bejeweled costume changes nightly[2] with 250 custom Louboutins[3] along

2   Glover, A. (2024, September 4). Here's how Taylor Swift changes outfit so quickly, and it's genius. HuffPost UK. https://www.huffingtonpost. co.uk/entry/taylor-swift-outfit-changes-speed-explained_uk_66d854ebe4b-0830f6e92e0a8

3   LeSavage, H. (2024, May 23). Taylor Swift has received more than 250 custom pairs of Louboutins for the ERAS Tour. Marie Claire. https://www. marieclaire. com/fashion/taylor-swift- custom- louboutins-eras-tour/

with the lighting and dance numbers during a recent pop music tour.

These next two stories make this point that owning and strategically controlling your video content is your success strategy. One made an enormous amount of money with video and the second one could have, but had a missed opportunity instead.

Story #1: Netflix

Unless you have been living in a cave for the past few decades you know about a company called Netflix. They disrupted the home entertainment market by launching a DVD-by-mail subscription service and later pivoted to on-demand streaming technology, leveraging customer data analytics to personalize recommendations and boost retention. Initially, they licensed popular movie and television content from Disney and other studios before producing original shows and movies to differentiate their catalog and reduce dependence on third-party content. Through aggressive international expansion and capturing market share from traditional video rental and cable companies, Netflix became the dominant player in the streaming entertainment industry. Another way to say it is that they licensed content from the big players, learned how to do it themselves and then became a source for consumer entertainment directly, rapidly dropping most of the licensing deals (and the payouts to them as well) like a bad date. Those big players like Disney and cable TV networks were left surprised and with less revenue. They came to rely on the license payments from Netflix, not realizing it was a Trojan horse to get in the castle, then they would be left behind. Those former giants are still struggling to figure out next steps in the digital era.

This history is important because it provides context. Is Netflix implementing the same playbook with podcasts? Recently Spotify and Netflix announced a deal that would enable some video podcasts on Spotify to be viewed on Netflix.[4] Netflix has just inked other similar deals with other media companies and recently engaged in an executive search for someone to head the entire podcast division. They have stated they

---

4   Spotify video podcasts head to Netflix under new distribution tie-up. (2025b, October 14). www.reuters.com. Retrieved October 18, 2025, from https://www.reuters.com/business/media-telecom/spotify-video-podcasts-head-netflix-under-new-distribution-tie-up-2025-10-14/

are also going to be offering live video podcasts.[5] These companies are combining to take your cow. "As video podcasts continue to grow in popularity, our partnership with Spotify allows us to bring full video versions of these top shows to both Netflix and Spotify audiences," said their vice president of content licensing and programming strategy.[6] They admit this is an area that is going to keep growing. They see the goldmine and it is you as the platforms you give your content to line up to do licensing deals with business partners to make more and more money from your content, while the average podcaster makes little to nothing at the end of the day with these deals.

Story #2: Andrew the Piano Teacher

I share this story with complete respect for the talented human it is about. He gave away the cow and did not earn nearly as much wealth as he could have, and should have, from what he gave to the world (and me). His story appears as a business case study here so you can learn from it. His name is Andrew Furmanzeck. He created videos that teach piano.

Once upon a rapidly growing YouTube early on people were posting about themselves and their hobbies and interests, and everything it seemed. A few years back when my beautiful mother died I started playing piano just to get my mind off of the deep pain. I found Mr. Furmanczyk's piano tutorials on YouTube which had millions of views. I found "How to play piano: The basics, Piano Lesson #1" which has a count of 28 million views and over 243,000 likes and growing.[7] He, in fact, has over 9 videos that have garnered over a million views each. Unassuming, unpolished and with hair bolder than Beethoven, he is possibly the best piano teacher

5 Spotify video podcasts head to Netflix under new distribution tie-up. (2025b, October 14). www.reuters.com. Retrieved October 18, 2025, from https://www.reuters.com/business/media-telecom/spotify-video-podcasts-head-netflix-under-new-distribution-tie-up-2025-10-14/

6 Spotify video podcasts head to Netflix under new distribution tie-up. (2025, October 14). www.reuters.com. Retrieved February 4, 2026, from https://www.reuters.com/business/media-telecom /spotify-video-podcasts-head-netflix-under-new-distribution-tie-up-2025-10-14/

7 Andrew Furmanczyk. (2008, July 10). How to play piano: The basics, Piano Lesson #1 [Video]. YouTube. https://www.youtube. com/watch?v=vphWgqbF-AM

out there for beginners. Not to mention he is likable, fun to listen to and watch. I learned the basics immediately and got an immense amount of enjoyment watching the video tutorials at the same time.

While many of his videos captured the attention of the masses with millions and millions of views and he later worked on developing an app, and has had more than one website, I looked for a way to sign up and connect with him directly and could not find another place where he and his tutorials were. All of the good stuff I wanted was freely available on YouTube and there was no other place to go to him directly for any content. Over half a million other people freely subscribed to his YouTube channel as well. I consumed what I wanted, took notes and screenshots for my own personal use to refer back to. I appreciated his tutorials and tried to find a way to pay him but could not. I looked at his app when it came out but it was clunky and did not offer anything I wanted.

What was great about him was that he was humble and authentic. He was clearly not in it for the money and just wanted others to learn. He was passionate about sharing his knowledge and thoughts on the subject . He was an expert in his videos and was a natural storyteller. The definition of a great teacher! It made for great content.

This was before other website platforms that encouraged paid subscriptions for meaningful, additional content became significant and widely used.

Mr. Furmanczyk stopped uploading videos on that YouTube channel over a decade ago. YouTube continues to draw large audiences to his videos. There is no public information on what YouTube (parent company Alphabet) paid Mr. Furmanzek and there were no headlines about large payouts either like the one Mr. Beast got when YouTube gave him $54 million in 2021.[8] He had health issues and took another job according to his social media posts at the time,[9] suggesting his payouts from You-Tube were considerably less than Mr. Beast and the other top contributors. With 525,000 subscribers, 65,721,607 video views and 201 uploaded videos to YouTube one source suggests Mr. Furmanzek was paid $2 for the

8   Brown, A., & Freeman, A. (2022b, May 12). The Highest-Paid You-Tube stars: MrBeast, Jake Paul and Markiplier score massive paydays. Forbes. https://www.forbes.com/sites/ abrambrown /2022/01/14/the-highest-paid-youtube-stars-mrbeast-jake-paul-and-markiplier-score-massive-paydays/
9   Furmanczyk, A. (n.d.). Biography. howtoplaypiano.ca. https://howto-playpiano.ca/bio/

month of February, 2024.[10]

Until the big hack we were on the platform Discord together in a piano group. I had the pleasure to thank him but I would have liked to subscribe to his teachings and put that money in his pocket. To my understanding all of his YouTube links in his channel description are now dead links . Yet of course, YouTube still makes money on his content that continues to draw an audience.

The point of this story is that if he had set up his activities from the start to provide only teasers on the platform that has made billions off of his and other creatives' content, and possibly a subscription on a personal website for more content, I would have gladly joined up. At just $5 a person a month even with that many subscribers he would have earned life changing money. It was his content. He set it up to share out of the goodness of his being. The platform took it and made money from it, giving him virtually nothing back.

Once the content was out and had garnered all of those views it was too late to reign it back in and regrow it, guiding viewers to a learning app or other website for the videos. You get one good chance when a rocket launches to be in the seat with your seatbelt fastened and ready to go. To this day he seems to be happy that he has given so much to so many people and for that we thank him. I still wish I could have financially contributed more to him for the content he created.

Sales. Sales. Sales. They are yours for the taking. What these two stories highlight is that if you set up your side hustle podcast business activities properly at the start before millions of adoring fans and supporters find you, like you and consume your entire content you can direct the fortunes like a modern day pop star. If you have made it and people like it and pay for it, why shouldn't these profits be yours?

It actually gets even more insulting today for creatives like Andrew and others who have uploaded their content to these platforms because YouTube content is allegedly extensively used to train and power Large Language Models (LLMs) to assist Artificial Intelligence (AI). Technology companies, including Google and OpenAI, have utilized YouTube video transcripts, metadata, and captions to train AI models and AI is

10   Andrew Furmanczyk net worth, income and estimated earnings of Youtuber channel. (n.d.-b). YouTubers.me. https://gb.youtubers.me/lypur/youtube-estimated-earnings

the reason many people are being laid off. So not only are some creative contributors not being paid, their content is essentially being stolen, and if that wasn't unpleasant enough they are unintentionally supporting other humans getting laid off with the growth and feeding of AI as well![11]

"That's not fair" you say. "I never agreed to that" you think. Yes you did. In the fine print in those constantly changing lengthy "Terms of Service" documents in the footer section no one ever reads that you agree to be a slave to by using their platform and uploading your free content to them and when you first set up an account. Don't work free. Keep your best content and sell it yourself elsewhere. Give them enough crumbs to help you find your audience. Make those your personal Terms of Service. Like the credit card you pay off every month so you are using the service free, set up your side hustle podcast to use these platforms to make money rather than have the platforms use you to do so.

In summary, consumers want video and they are willing to pay for it. They can pay you and will if you set it up for them to do so or they can pay another business like a technology platform that is unlikely to fairly compensate you if you give it away to them. Be stealth and get your wealth from the start as you set up and grow your side hustle podcast.

Hollywood and the entertainment industry, including podcasting, has become fully democratized. What used to be an air tight huge sector of business where you couldn't even get past the secretary to get five minutes on the phone or in person with the powermongers is now blown wide open. An entire industry has been demolished, destroyed and is being rebuilt. Like a pinata that goes boof and stuff is flying in the air, you can catch some of this candy. Advertisers want to deal with you directly and give you their money. I am proof of this because it has happened to me with my podcast. Let them. Time to get ready for what will become your favorite word–"no." The next chapter teaches you why this is.

---

11   Ostwal, T., & Ostwal, T. (2026, January 26). EXCLUSIVE: YouTube overtakes Reddit as Go-To citation source on AI Search. Adweek. https://www.adweek.com/media/ youtube-reddit- ai- search-engine-citations/

CHAPTER 6
Pitch Perfect

Cut Through Every "No" and Find the Next "Yes"

Growing your podcasting empire is a long game. If you want instant success a lottery ticket is a lot less likely to cause victory, but a much faster path to financial success if you do hit. There will be some of your podcast episodes that will not catch on as much as others will. The good news is that no one but you sees the full results of any show. No one. No company or platform. Only you. And no one sees how many advertisers say no to you before you get those beautiful "yes" answers that fill up your business bank account with happiness.

This chapter is about dealing with rejection when selling and networking for success.

You wouldn't be human if you didn't dislike constantly hearing no as an answer and regularly working without making any big money at first. It gets extremely frustrating. I know it is shocking, but the world does not always see your brilliance the instant you put it out. They should.

They just should.

There is a long list of talented and famous celebrities who were told they would never make it. Oprah Winfrey was told she was "unfit for television" and even fired from her first news job. Walt Disney was reportedly dismissed from a newspaper for "lacking imagination." Michael Jordan was cut from his high school varsity basketball team, Keith Urban failed music class in high school, and J.K. Rowling faced rejection from a dozen publishers who insisted children's books didn't sell. Stephen King had Carrie rejected 30 times—so many that he threw the manuscript in the trash before his wife rescued it.

Others faced industry-level doubt. Beyoncé lost Star Search and was dropped by her first girl group long before becoming an icon. Albert Einstein's teachers thought he was slow and wouldn't amount to much. Elvis Presley was told by the Grand Ole Opry to "go back to driving a truck," and Steve Jobs was famously fired from Apple, the company he founded, by people who doubted his leadership. Lady Gaga was dropped by her first label after just three months, and Lizzo was repeatedly told she didn't have the right "look" for the music industry. The Beatles were rejected by Decca Records, who claimed "guitar groups are on the way out." Tyler Perry struggled for years as his early plays were ignored while he battled homelessness. Shonda Rhimes was told she wasn't "creator material," and Rihanna was mocked for her accent and told she would never succeed outside of Barbados. Each of these successful people proved their critics wrong in spectacular fashion. Many of them are authors who are alive today and are welcome on my hit podcast show–reach out to come on the show because we think you are great!

But wait, there is more. Volumes more. Howard Schultz was rejected by banks and investors who insisted Americans would never pay premium prices for coffee at a place called Starbucks. Even Airbnb's founders were told their idea was absurd because "strangers will never stay in each other's homes," forcing them to sell novelty cereal boxes just to survive. Richard Branson struggled with dyslexia and faced skepticism over his early Virgin ventures, when he was a virgin at it basically. The list is practically endless. It almost seems like a right of passage to make it for some bonehead to first tell you that you shouldn't quit your day job, you have no talent and you should shut up and go face the wall in the corner.

Every no is a stepping stone on the path to the next yes. Think about how exciting it is to get that next no and learn to want to hear it because it means you are now one more phone call or email or DM funnel closer to the next yes when you do! Lean into it. Learn to love the word no because it is your friend on the path to your next sales victory. Remember and embrace this. It makes the rejection so much easier by giving it a positive slant and turning it into a game.

For the hit podcast The Naughty Librarian when I started selling ads I had luck immediately. When I realized people were listening and liking my podcast episodes in Season 1 I decided to see if I could sell an advertisement on one of the episodes. This is a true story and I am not embellishing it. The first day I started to offer ads directly to other businesses I sold an ad on an episode from a total stranger, within 2 hours. I then sold 2 more in that first week.

Those sales were sweet money right into the bank through the website. I delivered. Advertisers got what they wanted in the episodes. It was a win-win. I grew it.

If I didn't have it to sell I couldn't make money from it and I couldn't give those entrepreneurs the opportunity to also reach more people directly and impactfully with their business message. So I was actually doing those businesspeople a service by selling to them. They would have had to spend a lot more to pay for less effective ads that were less likely to be heard and seen in other places like radio. They would have to pay more for the same spot on my podcast if they had purchased through any of the podcast directories we were on including Spotify and Apple Podcasts. Yes, some platforms also put ads before and after my podcast episodes I upload to them, but no one gets in the content or anywhere in the entire half hour episode without going directly through me to buy. Those platforms could not even rip out my embedded ads if they tried because they are part of the conversation in my episodes, the storytelling. They would have to edit out the content or delete the episodes entirely to do so.

This is building stealth wealth, and immensely effective by directly selling to the companies that want to advertise and reach your target market. It is called business-to-business (B2B) selling. Make sure you clearly let them know how effective this type of ad is when you start offering your ad space for episodes and are cutting through the no responses to get to the next yes. People listen to ads that do not sound like ads and do sound like entertainment. Ours do not sound like ads unless the advertiser wants them to.

That said, do not keep trying to sell something to someone who does not want it. There are typically four main requirements for a successful sale. B.A.N.T. is an acronym that stands for Budget, Authority, Necessity or Need and Timeline. Those four ingredients are usually required for every sale you will ever make.

Budget. The buyer must have the money to buy it. Lots of businesses want to advertise. Only some have the resources in their budget to do so. Unless you are giving a few away to start for appearances or to be nice to companies you like, avoid companies you know have no budget to spend on advertising when reaching out to sell. Note that I have also bartered with other businesses and that is an option sometimes when a business does not have a lot of cash but does have something you would like in return and wants an ad.

Authority. You need to be communicating with the person who has the authority to buy the ad or whatever it is you are selling. A child might want a toy but the parent holds the wallet. The child can convince the parent, but the one with the money makes the final decision. Aim as high up on the organization's hierarchy as you can and in the right department so you are reaching the person who is able to say yes to your sales pitch or pass it down to the right person to do so. By doing so you will be wasting less time and having fewer unsuccessful conversations to get your ad space sold.

Need. Necessary. The prospect may have the budget and you may be speaking to the right person but if they do not think they need what you are selling they will not buy your ad space at any price. They need to believe it is necessary for them. This does not mean it actually is. It just means they think it is. Do they have the same target market as you do in your listeners? Then they might perceive they need the advertising you have for sale to get in front of them.

Timeline. If they have the budget, and you are speaking with the right person and they have decided they want what you have to offer but the timing is not right you cannot close a sale. Timing works in your favor and timing can work against you. If you want to get a job at a college and your chosen state or province just laid off 10,000 college professors due to poor economic times, read the room, it is a much harder gig to secure. This is true for sales. If the next company budget does not come out for several months and they already spent their allotment of funds you cannot not get a sale until the money is available for them to spend unless they do something drastic with their plans and budget. If, however, they are cash rich or have just had a windfall and have a huge marketing budget as your call comes in, you are much more likely to close that sale.

To help your timing you can convey a sense of urgency to the other party. You can let a prospective buyer know why they need to buy now, not in a few weeks or months. Possibly it is because there is an episode about to air with a topic or guest they would benefit by being linked to? Perhaps because you are offering a discount but only this week? Do they have a new product coming out in 2 months and want to buy an ad or guest star on your podcast to coincide with this launch? Do your homework and you might get a sale based on your knowledge and research around this timing.

A wonderful sales technique exists to cut through every "No" and find the next "Yes." It does not have one specific name but it is most commonly referred to as "No Counting" or "Counting Your No's." Top ad salespeople and streaming media reps swear by this technique. It is brilliant and effective.

In this selling survival technique you turn the entire process into a mathematical reality, a simple game. It helps eliminate the emotion and anxiety that goes with rejection in the sales process. This is the idea behind it: instead of fearing rejection, you actively track every "No" you get. Each rejection isn't wasted—it's a learning step that helps you understand how much effort it takes to get a "Yes," and it also makes that "Yes" feel more valuable. Here is how it works.

You are selling advertising space on an episode of your podcast show. You call, message or email 10 companies to see if they want to advertise. Nine of them say "No, we're not interested," and only one says "Yes." At first, hearing so many "No's" might feel discouraging. But in this sales technique, each "No" actually has value—it helps you understand how much the "Yes" is worth.

Here's why: every time a company says "No," you learn something. Maybe their budget is too small, maybe they're advertising elsewhere, or maybe your pitch wasn't clear enough. Each rejection is giving you information about the BANT. It also gives you practice refining your pitch, so the next company you talk to is more likely to say "Yes." When a company finally buys advertising space, that "Yes" is not random—it's the result of all the learning and effort that came from the "No's."

To see it in numbers, suppose selling one ad slot earns $1,000 as was the case for one type of ad in the second season of the podcast The Naughty Librarian. If it took 10 "No's" to get 1 "Yes," you can think of each "No" as a step toward earning that $1,000. Each of those answers gets you 10% closer to the yes in this case. It is a moving average and not exact, but you get the idea. Each "No" is like an investment: you deal with the rejection, but realize it helps you get closer to the big payoff. The more "No's" you count and learn from, the more you understand how much effort is needed to land a "Yes," and how valuable that "Yes" really is. After several sales you can calculate an average number of rejections that lead to successful sales.

This technique also changes your mindset. Instead of fearing rejection, you start seeing "No's" as part of the process. Every rejection is not a failure—it's information to improve your pitch and approach. It is a springboard to the next successful sale. Professional salespeople use this method to stay motivated and to get better over time, knowing that each "Yes" becomes more valuable because of all the "No's" that led to it. In short, when selling advertising space on your active podcast, this technique is about tracking every rejection, learning from it, and understanding that each "Yes" is worth much more because of the effort behind it. The word "No" has immense value and you want to hear it!

In addition to understanding the key elements to driving a sale and knowing you are worth it despite any negative responses, and realizing a "No" answer has value by turning it into a math game, another sales survival technique in dealing with rejection is to laugh about it. Use a recording technique I call "the idiot factor." The joke becomes on them and you keep stepping toward success. This is really helpful when the no responses are unkind, and that happens.

I developed this tool on my way to my first big paycheck early on in sales. I wrote down the most creative rejections. I used to wallpaper my wall with physical rejection letters before the days of email rejections, and then burn them when the next big success moment came. All those people listed earlier who did not see what the rest of the world would see in Oprah, Elvis, and others, while they are missing it are lovingly referred to as the idiots (privately only, of course).

You can start your own word document, put them on post-it notes stuck to your wall or write it out old school in a lined binder and literally record 'the tale of the tape' like a battle royale. Then destroy them or remove them so you have a blank wall or page for the next round when you reach a "yes" response. Instead of hurting you, let rejection entertain you by recording it and controlling it. You are making this list so you can laugh about it later on your own when you are hugely successful. They sure missed out on you!

Here are some of my idiot list recordings from recent ad sales communications for my podcast.

"Hard pass. Take us off of your mailing list." (I had no 'mailing list: it was all authentic one-on-one communication. One more no from a hoodie billionaire founder and CEO directly on the way to my next yes.)

"I just don't see the connection." (Dude, you have commercials everywhere on traditional radio that everyone turns down or off including myself. Whatever. I've been rejected by bigger businesses than yours…). I was one step closer to the next "yes."

I am going to try to add a few more here before this book goes to press. I seem to be getting less rejection and more kindness when it occurs though, which is good. Success begets further success.

Rinse, repeat. Rinse, repeat, take a breath, don't over eat. Self care. Self love. Get back on the horse. Laugh out loud at those who do not see the obvious opportunity. Next.

It is a fact of life that life is sales. It is a fact of sales that you can get everything right, but until and unless you have BANT, a thick skin, some survival techniques and a sense of humor about it all so you can keep forging forth selling ads and other offerings as a podcaster, the journey to success is going to be a cold ride on a dirty bus seat for awhile. Just keep pitching.

Rejection is redirection. Rejection is protection. If it is for you it will not pass by you. These are some great sayings that are true, and will help you when someone else does not immediately see your brilliance and say "yes" to the opportunity you present them. How you frame it is how you will make it. Churn, burn and earn. Make your mantra and stick to it. This is another technique that works as you wade through the sewage spill of rejection. There are so many great tips and techniques to maintaining a healthy attitude when wading through the rejection that comes with selling that I have compiled a short list of survival tips here you can quickly refer back to. These help you focus on success.

The 7 Sales Survival Tips for Success:

1.   Know Your Numbers: Highlight download stats, audience demographics, and engagement metrics (see that chapter) to show real value to potential sponsors.

2.   Tailor Every Pitch: Research each business and show how your podcast aligns with their target audience—one-size-fits-all pitches rarely succeed.

3.   Focus on Solutions, Not Ads: Explain how sponsoring your podcast solves a marketing problem for them, instead of just asking for money.

4.   Leverage Social Proof: Use testimonials, listener feedback, or past sponsorship success stories to build credibility.

5.   Follow Up Strategically: Persistence matters—send polite follow-ups with additional value rather than repeated generic requests. If they have said to call them back three times it usually means no and they are unable to say it. Leave it up to them to call you in case they purchase later.

6.   Build Relationships: Treat advertisers and sponsorships as partnerships, not transactions; long-term relationships are more profitable than one-off deals.

7.   Stay Confident and Positive: Your attitude influences results—confidence and professionalism make brands more likely to invest.

Another great sales (and life) technique is to develop and use mantras. A mantra is a short, repeated, and actionable phrase or belief that guides one's mindset and behaviors. Write these mantras somewhere and poster them in your house (the bathroom?). Refer to them anytime you want a boost. Use these or make your own. They are powerful tools to help you.

- I can accomplish anything if I do not give up.
- Someone has to have the next big podcast, why not me?

- A growth mindset that wins means I know that.
- I can learn more from mistakes than I can from success.
- Celebrate every victory.
- I'm going to risk it to get the biscuit.
- The person responsible for my success is the person I am looking at in the mirror.
- Today is another chance to achieve my goals and dreams.

The best way to handle rejection in sales is to actually have success. Nothing feeds the effort like positive feedback and wins. It feels great and encourages you to keep going. Take time to celebrate all victories, great and small.

One way I have obtained incredible sales success is through the professional network LinkedIn. It is one of the reasons the podcast The Naughty Librarian "TNL" did as well as it did right out of the gate in its first year. For this reason, since I want you to succeed and it is a repeatable formula, it is discussed as a section in this chapter to teach you what you need to know to use it to your advantage.

Networking on LinkedIn

They do not pay me to say this but everyone except a few aristocrats needs to be on LinkedIn. Use the free version. There is no need to pay for most podcasters. It can become pricey for the beginning entrepreneur podcaster to get a paid subscription and it is not usually necessary.

LinkedIn is a platform under Microsoft. When in the process of selling, one single no response on this platform is worth about a thousand no answers in real life everywhere else put together. This is because it is so streamlined with professionals who are authentic with legitimate, verifiable accounts, have a spending allowance for marketing, and are engaging there for their business. That said, do not be transactional right away when you get started using the platform if you are new to it. Be human.

You want to start your free, basic account on this professional networking platform as soon as possible because the older your account is the more credibility you have and the more likely people are to believe you are sincere when you connect with them. You are in business after all, so you deserve to have a presence there.

Set your profile with your brand in mind. The banner and photo space of your profile should be filled so it looks professional. Have the images be on-brand for you and your podcast. If you are between jobs or looking while you are growing your side hustle podcast you can be extremely general in your employment details. Less is more on the information you list about yourself for all kinds of reasons. Do not give out exact information when completing the sections because you do not need any unwanted followers coming to your door in real life. Note that there are a lot of fake jobs listed on this platform with no real job offer behind them so double check any listings externally before applying and submitting your resume if you are searching for additional work while you are building your podcast.

You want to be on this platform because this professional business network is full of executives who own and run companies that might want to partner with you and buy your podcast episode ads as you grow. It is a platform full of people who will potentially say yes to you. You might find guests, new listeners, new crew members, friends, and other important people on this platform in addition to the business people you can interact with for your podcast and business. On this platform you can connect directly with many of them.

I have sold ads and found great podcast episode guests and new listeners directly through posts and DM funnels (explained below) on this platform. That said, I am always authentic. I often say when I reach out that my message is not spam so the person knows. Avoid being a spammer here. If you try, you will get found out and possibly blocked or removed quickly.

To grow your network, ask for a connection. Accept all reasonable connection requests and reach out regularly to people to make more. It is easy to spot fakes, thankfully. They usually have newly made accounts with few or no photos. Do not be afraid to block or remove someone if they have a brand new account or do not say much, or say something on a post or a message you do not like. You have the power. If someone starts spamming I remove them right away and encourage you to do the same.

This platform is currently one of the best available anywhere to reach an intelligent, aware and sincere audience for your podcast if that is your goal. My podcast listeners and guests are thinkers, many are educated and are successful professionals. On this platform, unlike many others, there is no need to constantly post if you do not want to because that is not the game here for most people. Do not take it personally if there is no reach back or connect back when you send a message or connection request because sometimes people set up accounts and then rarely log in. Just move on to the next one. A lot of people do actively log in and check their messages and respond when they think it is real and worthwhile.

So get started on this platform if you are not yet already on it. If you are, add or update your profile with your personal brand choices, with new professional photographs. Have a general biography that impresses strangers enough that they might want to follow you back and check out your podcast. Obviously include details of your new podcast with links to listen and follow.

This addition to my social media strategy is one of the reasons my podcast went global quickly. Other platforms can offer similar levels of growth, but do not have the same user authenticity. With minimal time and direct messaging this platform can be powerfully effective.

A LinkedIn DM funnel is a systematic approach to generating leads and sales by guiding prospects through stages (Awareness, Nurture, Convert) using valuable content and personalized direct messages, turning profile views and content engagement into booked calls or paid customers, often starting with broad outreach and narrowing down to direct conversations. It combines content (posts, videos) to attract attention with targeted DMs to build relationships, solve problems, and offer solutions, ultimately aiming to convert followers into paying clients. It is a strong tool to grow your podcast.

Key Stages of a LinkedIn DM Funnel:

Awareness (Top of Funnel):
- Goal: Attract a broad audience and introduce your brand/expertise.
- Tactics: Share high-visibility, valuable content (insights, stories, industry tips) to get impressions and attract followers. Pin to your profile in order of strength so you do not need to continue to post much or at all.
- DM Action: Send initial, personalized DMs to new followers saying hello, asking why they followed and what challenges they face or

something similar and appropriate.

Nurture (Middle of Funnel):
- Goal: Build trust and demonstrate value.
- Tactics: Offer educational content, case studies, webinars, or lead magnets (checklists, guides) to deepen engagement.
- DM Action: Engage in conversations, address specific problems, and offer more tailored resources, moving from broad content to deeper discussions.

Conversion (Bottom of Funnel):
- Goal: Turn engaged prospects into listeners, clients, or sales.
- Tactics: Use clear Calls-to-Action (CTAs) in posts and DMs, highlight success stories, or offer promotions or other benefits.
- DM Action: Guide the conversation towards booking a call, obtaining a media kit, or making a purchase, framing it as the natural next step in the relationship, not a hard sell.

How it Works in Practice:
- Content as Bait: Your public posts act as the "one-to-many" attraction, getting people interested. Always pin the best ones.
- DMs as the Hook: When someone interacts (follows, engages), you use personalized DMs to pull them into a one-on-one conversation, a "one-to-one" method.
- Problem Solving: The focus shifts from broadcasting to actively helping solve their specific business problems, making the transition to an offer feel natural.

In essence, it's about using content to get attention and DMs to build the relationship, leading to a conversion, all while feeling helpful and authentic rather than using an overt sales pitch. This funnel technique can be used to authentically engage in a meaningful way to grow your business and podcasting goals.

If you are new to the platform or do not have much of a following yet reach out and if you are legitimate we may follow you back. It is always advisable to support your connections back with following, listening and giving 5-star ratings and reviews if you like, and commenting on posts or messaging to further build relationships online. See the section at the end of this book entitled "How to Stay in Touch with Me" to find where I currently am on this and other platforms. Let's help each other continue to grow and thrive. Let's become the next business "yes" for one another. I'm in.

CHAPTER 7
Editing to Launch
Creating Your Sunshine

Once you've recorded your podcast episode meeting it is time to edit the raw files and perform adjustments so you can turn it into the final version that you launch and sell ads on. It is time to create your sunshine. You are now in the "post-production" stage aka "post." It is in this stage where you organize your episode contents, enhance the sound and improve the overall quality. This is where the magic happens!

Post production can be boring and time consuming but it is also the most powerful part of your workflow to shape your entire creative message. That sentence you couldn't spit out the first five times? Rip it out and save it as a year-end blooper. You'll sound better without it in the main episode. A guest made a blunder and you are not presenting the episode live? Extract it and you have another blooper. I like to make my guests sound their best with gentle editing as needed. I do not change who they are or how they speak but do ensure I put them in their best light. I ask myself what I would want, and treat them the same way.

In editing the entire raw file you want to select the most engaging portions to turn them into short teaser clips, behind-the-scenes content, still images and any other related content you require for your 12 Month Marketing and Social Media Strategy you developed in your Business Plan in Chapter 2. You also edit the recorded footage to make the full-length audio podcast to the length you have selected. In that file you will add your placeholder and distribute it as a video file with just the audio and that image. Of course, you also edit into your episode any commercials that have been sold.

This chapter grows your editing knowledge so you can do it yourself if you want to instead of hiring someone else to do it, which is also an option if you have the budget and interest to do so. Editing is a skill. It is creative, so some artistic people tend to like doing it because of the control it gives them over the tone and voice of the final product. I find it fun and tedious. The podcast The Naughty Librarian does very little editing overall since we like the authentic conversation approach which the listeners seem to enjoy as well.

To get started honing your superpower editing skills this chapter introduces you to editing software, basic editing techniques and related post-production preparation required to distribute your podcast show and its related social media short clips everywhere it should go. This includes finalizing your cover art, thumbnails, and show notes with effective copy using keywords for discoverability. For this understanding, Search Engine Optimization (SEO) for podcasts which is called Podcast Search Engine Optimization (PSO) is also explained.

Don't worry if you haven't done any editing before. If you can cut, tape, and wrap a present you can learn to edit. Many affordable programs with user friendly interfaces exist to make the job of editing extremely easy since we live in a video filled world.

Editing Software
Editing is not only important, it is a critical step in producing a successful podcast. It enables you to have professional, exciting podcast episodes others can enjoy. The first step to proper editing is choosing good editing software that meets your needs and budget. I have professional editing software on my desktop computer at home that I never see because I am always traveling with the podcast these days but my low-cost high-impact editing software on my travel laptop works great. None

of the companies behind the products and services listed in this section paid me to include them here. I specifically did not allow them to sponsor this work so you know the information you are receiving is authentic, unbiased advice.

Let me start with two tips. First, I discourage you from using editing tools on platforms you will upload your podcast episodes to such as Spotify and Apple Podcasts. Apple, for example, is launching new editing tools as this book goes to print.

Why? Two reasons. First, because you want control over access to your video now and in the future and by doing so it limits their access to it. You do not want them to change their Terms of Use later in a way that you do not agree with and then have to remove your content if it has grown an audience there. The way to use them to your advantage is to limit their access to your content. What they do not have, they cannot take. Second, you do not want to use their editing software because there are better options available at affordable prices. Your time is money and you want to use the easiest, best options possible while keeping control of the contents and creating professional quality.

For post production I have learned and used several software programs over the years. For larger projects like movies and streaming shows professionals use video editing programs offered by Avid, Adobe, Final Cut Pro, and others, which are all excellent. Some have a free trial and then you pay for a subscription. These professional programs enable robust handling of multi-hour projects and have collaborative capabilities. This extends far beyond what a podcaster requires so unless you want to invest considerable time and money to become a professional video editor these options are more than you need.

For extensive everyday editing with professional quality at a great price I currently use the video editing software offered by CyberLink PowerDirector since it is reliable and affordable with lots of creative tools and fast performance. It has never let me down. It works great with no need to buy any of the additional features or credits and is available for both Windows and Mac environments.

Whatever software you choose, avoid any free trials that leave a watermark on your video. Usually you get what you pay for and free is unlikely to be a sufficient option for the serious podcaster who also makes video clips to promote the show.

Editing basics

Once the recording session (the 'sesh') is complete, depending on the video conference platform you have selected and how you have set it up beforehand, you may need to convert the file to a file format such as an MP4 file so that you can import it into your editing software and manipulate it there. Look at the settings in the program you chose to find out how to do this as every platform is slightly different. When you end the meeting and receive a pop-up message that the file is saving and converting, let it finish without closing any windows or engaging in any other activity on your device. This ensures a clean capture and complete process. It could take awhile if the interview was a long one. Walk away, get a cup of tea, call a friend, just be patient and wait so you do not accidentally do anything to corrupt the file. Video files are large files. They take a minute. You do not want to lose the meeting you just completed.

After conversion it is a good habit to save the raw file immediately. I put it in the cloud to eliminate single device risk. Again, let this upload completely and wait before closing windows and files as the back end of the video transfer needs to catch up, even if it appears to be completed. Sometimes a message saying a file is uploaded really means it is almost done and if you close everything out and turn off your computer too soon you can go back later and get a nasty error message saying that the file is not there. Do not learn this the hard way. I personally do not delete working files until a season is over and I never delete original raw files.

After your raw file is in the proper file format on your computer and saved into drive as well if you wish, you import it into your digital audio workstation (DAW) or your preferred podcast editing software, whatever you have chosen. There you can manipulate each track or section of video and audio individually and apply detailed processing as much or as little as you choose. You may need to export the audio (if applicable) using lossless formats like WAV or AIFF rather than compressed formats, if required. All MP4 files should be able to be imported correctly into most editing software.

For the professionals who are using more than basic video editing software with a simple interface perform phase alignment and noise reduction selectively if desired, as conferencing software often introduces subtle artifacts. Normalize levels across tracks and apply consistent gain staging before adding dynamics processing or equalization. You can maintain detailed session logs during recording production—including sample rates, bit depth, and routing paths—so that future recordings can replicate the optimal configuration and avoid recurring technical pitfalls should you need them.

For user friendly video editing software used by most podcasters it is simpler to get started. Your setup includes something like Zoom plus CyberLink PowerDirector video editing software on your laptop or desktop and some cloud storage like Google Cloud. The basics along with some tips and tricks are explained next. Once you have selected your software and have started using it you can delve more deeply into learning more advanced editing techniques after these basics are mastered. Since there are so many software options to choose from it is impossible to go into advanced detail here. This section is general information only. You are encouraged to view any tutorials that may be offered after you purchase your editing software. Companies often provide them and tell you about them in emails they send you with links because they want you to have a good experience with their product you have purchased, so you will continue to buy it. Use this good information as a great place to start your learning.

The first step in editing when you have imported your file(s) into your chosen editing software and are ready to splice and dice the contents to get that final episode is to listen to your entire recording. Edit for content on your first listen and work on noise issues or other distractions on your second pass. If you focus on noise issues too soon, you might polish sections you remove later anyway. If you don't want to listen to an entire episode multiple times, create a list with a time meter (this is sometimes called a "log" or "punch-list") of audio distractions, major issues and other key moments to check during your second review. You can also create markers with comments in the timeline if your editing software allows for this, like PowerDirector does.

When assessing the overall audio quality listen for technical issues: volume inconsistencies, noise, dropped words. Tracks may have discrepancies due to different microphone setups or room acoustics so you might want to balance audio levels between participants. Use gain adjustments or a volume automation tool if available to even out levels and ensure each speaker is clearly audible without distortion.

Before cutting the whole recording into segments and adjusting them individually, consider boosting or lowering the entire volume of the whole uncut clip you dragged to the timeline of your editor first if it needs it and the entire level is significantly off in some way. It is easier to boost or lower all of it at one time and just alter any clips that still end up being too hot (volume too high) or soft than to do this for each individual segment you have created if it is all markedly off. If you have captured the recording at an optimal volume with only short sections significantly too loud or too quiet then this step is not required. You can strategically make ranges and alter just those segments. Normalize to target loudness (e.g., –16 LUFS). Look at where the levels are relative to the maximum line before distortion starts to occur. Get a friend to listen and look with you if you are not sure what the best loudness is. Trust your own ears. Over time as you continue to edit you will get better at recording and editing for optimal volume.

Be careful to not move or rename files on your computer when you are editing because for many nonlinear editing programs doing so will break a required link to the file which can prevent the program from being able to use it. You would then have to find the file and repeat your work. Avoid deleting files for the same reason. The editing process does not actually change the original files on your computer, it just refers to them for their information. When they are moved or changed it cannot do so.

Once you have a punch list, markers, or have listened carefully and have identified problem areas in the recording you should remove large chunks of the session you know you do not want. Trim silence, pauses, or excessive filler words that do not add value unless you do not have a long enough recording. This helps maintain pacing and keeps the audience engaged. Online meeting recordings often capture natural gaps between speakers, which can be tightened to create a more cohesive listening experience.

Since recordings often contain hum, fan noise, or other environmental sounds noise reduction can be applied using a plug in or the tools in your editor. It is advisable to clean the audio a bit, but avoid over-processing, which can make voices sound unnatural or hollow.

When you cut portions of audio, you can sometimes get small pops or clicks in the finished mix. Use the fade tool at the beginning and end of segments if you run into those glitches to remove these unwanted sounds. You could also add an interesting short sound like a musical instrument note such as a triangle being struck or a tuba blowing a B flat. Make it your own. Be distinct and find your editing style.

Equalization (EQ) is a way to change how high or low sounds are so music or voices sound clearer and better. It can enhance clarity and presence. Remove unwanted low-end rumble and gently boost frequencies for speech clarity without harshness. Be careful with aggressive EQ adjustments, as they can alter the timbre of the voices and create listener fatigue over long episodes.

Compression is useful to manage dynamic range. It makes loud sounds quieter and quiet sounds louder so everything is easier to hear and more even. Some recordings may have peaks and valleys in volume as speakers move closer or farther from the microphone. Apply light compression to keep levels consistent while preserving the natural dynamics of conversation. You want to ensure you preserve natural conversation dynamics you have captured.

Editing content flow is just as important as technical processing. Listen for timing and pacing issues. Recording sessions can include overlaps or awkward interruptions. Cut redundant statements, adjust the placement of segments and remove any jarring transitions to maintain a smooth rhythm that feels natural to the listener. I had one episode where the guest was incredibly talented and well spoken but spoke so fast it was difficult to understand. I reduced the speed slightly so it was in the normal range for a listener. It was a subtle, yet needed update or the entire episode would have failed.

Consider inserting light sound effects, or transitions to enhance narrative structure. Be creative and add music you own or have the rights to use if you want. Less tends to be more with extra sounds as they can be distracting.

Finally, quality control. Once you have the final episode of your podcast ready to upload and unleash to the world you need to check your results. Always review sample segments of the exported episode on multiple devices and environments, such as headphones, speakers, and mobile devices. This quality control step ensures your quality is sufficient and consistent so others can actually hear it. It confirms that your editing decisions translate well across listening scenarios and provides a professional experience for your audience. Once my episodes are dropped I immediately listen to them in full the moment they are live just in case I accidentally uploaded something else or it has some other major mistake. I can pull it, correct it and upload an updated file if necessary with relatively minimal damage if it happens quickly. So far, thankfully, nothing like this has occurred. Upload an updated file rather than delete an episode if this is ever needed so the date of the episode drop does not change.

When you are exporting your final file it is advisable to use a file name that clearly indicates to you what it is. An example: S01_E01_0001A.mp4 (for the first season and episode, audio only and this file is a video file format with the MP4 video extension). Make it clear in the filename whether it is the video with audio or just the final audio with placeholder since you want to save both and use some or all of them for different purposes later.

In the export process also be aware when uploading your episodes to directories (explained in a later chapter) that there are file length and size maximums. For the podcast The Naughty Librarian each episode is 30 minutes long and the final episode of each season is one full hour with occasional bonus material. When I went to upload the finale for Season 2, the one with the powerful and impressive guest Pulitzer Prize-winning poet Diane Seuss, it had a fun, tiny tail at the end after the outro (like a movie that has an extra scene after the credits). I found out when uploading this episode that those few extra seconds pushed it past the maximum file size limits for uploading an MP4. Using the challenge as an opportunity I split the episode in half and made a bonus last episode (and was uploading it on Christmas Day that year–I am committed to success!). I also did not put the normal opening audio since I wanted it a bit sublime due to the vibe of the guest and show, and so the conversation literally just continued to start the very last episode of what became a two-part series. It received great feedback, especially from some people who did not have much to do on that holiday and they said it was a great addition to their day. Accidents can be wins. Videos have maximum file sizes so that is another reason to keep them short.

Podcast editing is primarily for cleaning up the recordings and making basic adjustments to the structure. It is not like editing other streaming and entertainment content which aims to be more polished. Try to keep your editing process straightforward. If you focus too much on production, you'll get distracted. If you overproduce your episodes you are wasting time you could be spending on promoting your show and it might not sound as good. Less is more, yet enough is required. You will find your balance as an editor.

Cover Art / Thumbnails

For a podcast, the thumbnail is just a smaller version of the cover art. For social media posts and in other places, a podcast thumbnail is often a different image made to fit that platform's size and style, even though it may use the same logo or cover art. It can also use different art and photos and have different styles and sizes. So to be clear podcast art can be a thumbnail but not all thumbnails come from the podcast art you create. Podcast art was explained in Chapter 3 when discussing branding. Thumbnails will now be explained here since they are needed to launch your podcast episode on directories and for your social media strategy.

Thumbnails for Your Podcast

Just like your podcast cover art, you want to go for clarity, contrast, and instant recognition with your thumbnail for the show. You want consistency.

A podcast thumbnail is the small square image that represents a podcast across platforms. It's often the first thing a potential listener sees, acting like the show's visual handshake. Because thumbnails are displayed at very small sizes, they need to be simple, high-contrast, and instantly readable—usually featuring bold text, a clear focal point, and minimal clutter.

The thumbnail for the podcast should project the podcast's brand so listeners can quickly recognize it and understand the show's vibe. This means using the same color palette, fonts, logo style, and visual tone found in the podcast's website, social media account banners and profile images, cover art and other promotional materials. A comedy podcast might use bright colors and playful typography, while a true-crime show might lean into darker tones and more serious design choices. As detailed earlier, strong branding consistency builds trust and memorability over time. When your thumbnail looks and feels aligned with the show's content and personality, it sets clear expectations and makes the podcast easier to spot in a crowded feed. In short, the thumbnail isn't just decoration—it's a key branding tool that helps attract the right audience and reinforces the identity of the show. Take advantage of this opportunity to attract more people to the podcast with the thumbnail.

Most directories prefer the file to be under about 500 KB to 512 KB so it loads quickly and doesn't get flagged for being too large, although some platforms may accept slightly larger files.

Episode-specific thumbnails have the same square sizing and should meet the platform's minimum pixel dimensions and file requirements to display properly in podcast apps. Remember that designing the image at the higher end (e.g., 3000 × 3000 px) and then compressing it to stay under the file-size limit helps ensure clarity at all sizes.

Your cover art converted to a thumbnail can be effective and save time. That is your best option for your podcast show episode thumbnails.

Thumbnails for your social media strategy

Thumbnails with posts are a core part of hooking an audience on social media. Here they represent a great opportunity many people waste. You want to create new ones for each new post since the same image reproduced dozens of times is not interesting.

A thumbnail's job on a social media post is similar to that of a podcast show's cover art in a podcast directory. It is to stop the scroll. It must grab attention instantly and spark curiosity, because it is often the first and only chance to earn a click and a view. Clarity beats cleverness: one clear idea is more effective than multiple competing signals. Emotion and contrast matter, with strong expressions, tension, or curiosity cues consistently outperforming neutral visuals. The thumbnail and title must work together, where the image teases the idea rather than repeating the text or explaining everything. Above all, the thumbnail should promise value fast so the viewer immediately senses what they will gain by clicking and exploring further.

From a composition standpoint, like cover art, the thumbnail should contain one dominant subject only, cropped tightly so the subject fills most of the frame. There must be a clear focal point that remains recognizable even at small sizes. If text is used, it should be limited to very few words, ideally one to five, set in large, bold, high-contrast lettering that is readable on a phone screen. Full sentences should be avoided. Lately for social media posts text with a contrasting colored background is being used. Sometimes the text comes from the transcript of the conversation if that is what is occurring.

Visually, the design should rely on high contrast between the subject and the background, using either a simple background or heavy background blur. Lighting should be bright or intentionally dramatic, and clutter, logos, or fine details should be avoided since they do not translate well at small sizes.

From a technical perspective, the image should use a rectangular aspect ratio optimized for widescreen viewing, with a minimum resolution suitable for large displays. The image must be sharp, free of compression artifacts, and saved at a file size optimized for fast loading. A neat trick is to put solid, contrasting colored borders on the side of any image so the rectangular look is there along with an attention grabbing frame. This saves time and avoids the step of having to go into a photo editing program and make an image exactly to size specifications so it will fit properly.

Strategically, the thumbnail should be designed to create curiosity rather than provide an explanation. It should match the emotional hook of the content and be tested and iterated over time based on click performance. One way to get a lot of photographs is to take frame shots while video editing. Most editors have some way to make a photograph from any paused image in the video.

Podcast Show Notes with Checklist

Podcast show notes, also called the podcast description, should be written to attract new listeners to your show. These notes appear with your episode in podcast directories and next to it on your podcast site. High-quality notes help new listeners find your content more easily by improving overall accessibility and SEO/PSO which is explained below. You never want to leave this blank. It is your way to shout into the void saying what you have to offer to attract listeners.

Try to include essential elements in your notes: helpful links, ancillary resources, business contact details, and a short summary of the episode. This gives listeners context and makes your show more discoverable and engaging. Most major apps support some formatting within your episode text, but not all platforms do. Keep this in mind when styling your episode description. Be cautious if transcripts or chapter sections are automatically generated as controlling your content is critical for ownership and potential revenue.

To Build Podcast Show Notes:

1. Write a clear description – Staying on brand. Summarize your episode in a few sentences. Use as many words as the platform allows.

2. Include helpful links – Reference resources or related content mentioned. We include our website link to www.TheNaughtyLibrarian.ca and our social media account links.

3. Add ancillary info – Include guest biographies, social media handles, and other related notes.

4. Provide contact info – Make it easy for listeners to reach you without risking your safety.

5. Format carefully – Check how your notes appear across apps to ensure consistency and impact.

6. Use transcripts/chapter markers wisely – Only auto-generate these if you choose to. Maintain control. Optional, but this boosts PSO (explained below).

7. Keep SEO and PSO in mind – Use relevant keywords to improve discoverability.

Search Engine Optimization (SEO) and Podcast Search Engine Optimization (PSO)

Search Engine Optimization (SEO) is a way to help websites show up higher in Google or other search engines so more people can find them. It works by using the right words, titles, and links that match what people are searching for. Podcast Search Engine Optimization, or Podcast Search Optimization (PSO), is very similar but for podcasts instead of websites. PSO helps people find a podcast when they search on Apple Podcasts, Spotify, or other podcast platforms by using good episode titles, descriptions, and keywords. The main difference is that SEO is mostly for web pages, while PSO is mostly for audio/podcasting shows, but both are about making it easier for people to discover your content online.

In this process relevant keywords are used in your episode titles, descriptions, show notes, and on your podcast website to help new listeners find your content more easily. Keywords for a podcast show description are the important words or phrases people are most likely to type when searching for your episode or topic. They should naturally appear in your title, description, and tags—like the guest's name, awards, topics discussed, and themes of the show—so platforms like Apple Podcasts and Spotify can match your episode to listeners who are searching for those words. At present, this optimization also involves using keywords from voice searches, leveraging AI-powered voice search to generate recommendations, and accounting for platform-specific search algorithms.

You structure your content and digital presence so both humans and algorithms can understand it. Effective copy with keywords not only improves discoverability but also helps your podcast appear in related searches, increasing both your reach and engagement over time. This naturally grows the number of listeners for your show without you having to do any more work to attract them.

Successful PSO goes beyond keywords by improving listener engagement signals that platforms often use to rank content. Consistent publishing, strong branding, detailed show notes, and well-written episode descriptions help attract clicks and encourage subscriptions, reviews, and longer listening times. Together, these factors increase a podcast's visibility in search results, recommendations, and charts, ultimately helping creators reach new listeners and grow their audience.

Strong PSO makes it easier for people to discover your podcast organically, increases your audience, and helps you compete in a crowded market. With over half a million podcasts regularly available and more podcasters getting in the game every day, effective PSO is one of the most reliable ways to grow your listener base.

The 7 Steps to Solid Epsode PSO

1. Episode Titles: Use clear, descriptive titles that include keywords people might type when searching for topics related to your podcast. For example, instead of "Episode 12," use "Best Toothpaste Tips for

Healthy Teeth." Clear, searchable episode titles reach wider audiences.

2. Episode Descriptions & Show Notes: Write detailed descriptions with keywords naturally integrated. Include summaries, key points, timestamps, links to resources, and any guest names. This helps search engines and podcast apps understand the content. Detailed episode descriptions with relevant keywords help your podcast find more listeners.

3. Transcripts: Publishing full transcripts of your episodes on your website and show notes not only improves accessibility but also gives search engines a lot of text to index, boosting discoverability.

4. Website Optimization: Make sure your podcast website is fast, mobile-friendly, and uses clear navigation. Include structured data (like schema markup) so search engines can properly categorize your episodes.

5. Platform-Specific SEO: Different platforms have their own search algorithms. Optimize your episode and promotional content for Spotify, Apple Podcasts, Google Podcasts, YouTube, and others by using tags, categories, and relevant keywords.

6. Voice Search & AI Recommendations: Presently a lot of people find podcasts through voice assistants and AI-driven suggestions. Using conversational keywords and descriptive metadata increases your chances of appearing in these results.

7. Link Building & Backlinks: Promote your episodes through guest appearances, collaborations, blog posts, and social media as per your plan developed in Chapter 2. Backlinks to your website or episodes from reputable sources signal credibility and improve SEO rankings.

Consistency and engagement is a critical component to success. Regularly publish episodes by stating and following the consistent publishing schedule set in your business plan and communicated to your audience and encouraging listener engagement (e.g. comments, ratings, reviews, follows, likes, reposts, shares, website views and conversions) also signals to search engines and platforms that your podcast is active and relevant.

Everyone has their own process and approaches editing differently. Be bold and go forth editing your creation. It gets easier the more you do it. You will find your sunshine.

CHAPTER 8
Fledging and Flying
What to Do with the Finished Product

Your product is recorded, edited, finalized and ready to launch. Now what? Like a new chick in the safe, warm, comfortable nest it is time to drop out of it in full panic and fly or die. (A bit dramatic here, it is not quite that intense.) This chapter covers the logistics of podcast distribution, explaining and clarifying key concepts including podcast publication, distribution, podcast directories, podcast networks, and podcast hosts. It offers a simple, effective, powerful and affordable way to distribute your podcast show and its episodes.

Essentially all distribution is publishing, but not all publishing is distribution. Podcast publishing is the broader act of creating, uploading, managing, and releasing episodes as part of an ongoing show. It encompasses everything from decisions about content, branding, recording, editing, and uploading it online to writing show notes, scheduling, and making the episode available to listeners. Some people might refer to publishing as the entire process of taking a podcast from the concept or idea to a fully live, realized, and available entertainment option in the world as a show with episodes. It includes everything discussed up to this point and what is about to be explained in this chapter as well.

Podcast distribution is more narrow. It is a subset of publishing. Specifically it is the process of delivering your audio files to listening platforms and directories via feeds and other syndication methods.

Podcast Networks, Hosts, and Directories

A podcast network is a collective of multiple podcasts, usually sharing branding, marketing, sponsorship deals, or production resources. It is concerned with organization and promotion and does not always host the audio of podcasts. It's a bit like a radio show playing many different songs.

Not to be confused with a podcast host that hosts the show, a podcast host for distribution is a different kind of podcast host. The role of a podcast host business is to store your podcast audio files, generate a feed called an RSS feed, and distribute it to directories. Without a host, your podcast has no "home" online. It is a required step to going live. It is not always called a host. There are dozens of hosting platforms with different features and prices. There are a lot of third-party ones that act as middle players but you do not need them and can avoid them. To add to the confusion, hosts are sometimes called directories and directories are sometimes called hosts because they can also offer hosting services.

A podcast directory is a platform where listeners search for, subscribe to, and stream podcasts, usually by reading a feed from the host. Podcast directories let listeners search and listen to shows. They point to your host if they do not actually host your show (however some do). A podcast directory is like a big library or catalog where people can find podcasts to listen to.

Examples include Apple Podcasts and Spotify. Directories can sometimes let listeners subscribe. They can act as a discovery tool. If someone hears about the podcast The Naughty Librarian they can search by name in a directory and find the show.

The easiest way to approach all of this currently without overspending your time and money and ceding control to third-parties that may go bankrupt in a heartbeat and leave you stuck is to set up and manage just three accounts yourself with these three big players.

One of the accounts you want to set up to distribute your podcast properly is an RSS account (available at www.rss.com). You want to register and set up an account there because it is a powerful distribution platform. Many other hosts you could hire to do this essentially just put your show here. Once you have your account started and are logged in, go to your dashboard and go through the steps to start a new show. With your show set up you go through the steps to upload a new episode. Do so with your first episode with your ready-to-go cover art and related elements explained in the preceding chapters.

What is great about this platform is that once you have set up your show on it there is an easy and powerful way to submit the episodes to other wide reaching podcast directories. By navigating to the distribution tab you can select a number of these options. Some of these I prefer to have accounts with directly and upload load my shows there but if you want to save time and do not have a need for that you can select directories from here and they eventually, automatically become available in many of those other places as well. This is a fantastic way to reach a lot of potential listeners where they like to find their podcasts. An RSS feed delivers your show directly to other directories in a lot of places where people find their podcasts. It sends the list of all your episodes with titles, descriptions, and links to the audio.

The second account you want to set up directly to distribute your show is Apple Podcasts. Because it is one of the biggest platforms and has a lot of analytics to offer creatives you want to start an account there rather than just feed it through RSS. Remember you are uploading the audio only as a video file format with placeholders. Once logged in you let them know about your new podcast show. Approval for a podcast show can take as long as 24 hours, since Apple indicates the company performs a human review on each new submission. You'll get an email notification once your show has been approved. Then you can create new episodes and drag and drop the final Mp4 episode file in, add the rest of the details and publish it. Publishing at this point in the process means submitting it for distribution. The button is sometimes labeled "publish."

With your own Apple account you can monitor your show and gain insight into how users are listening to it. You have more control. You don't need an Apple ID to submit your podcast to Apple Podcasts at the time this book went to press. You used to. You may again in the future. The one constant about technology is that it is always changing and it moves fast.

Spotify introduced its directory in 2018 and is currently one of the largest podcast platforms, with about a third of all podcast plays. Separately, you also want to go to Spotify for Creators (currently typing this in your web browser takes you to it: www.creators.spotify.com) and start an account to set up your show and upload your show episodes there as well. I love how they say they have worldwide analytics when they do not. It is really a good analysis of where your Spotify listeners specifically are and what episodes they prefer. It does not reflect the total show listener activity beyond Spotify.

Distributing your episodes on Spotify is very similar to the other accounts but not exactly the same. You will learn the subtle differences once you start using it. They include the number of characters allowed in the description and some other minor differences. Note that Spotify changes things often so this information can update frequently. For now they call where creatives who have a podcast and want to upload it "Spotify for Creators." That is where you currently go to get an account, set up a show and drop episodes.

Spotify processes your submission before it goes live and there may be a wait until you can hear and see it as well. Note that if you accidentally have any copyrighted audio you cannot prove you have the right to use they will tear your hard work down in a red hot minute. Then you are wasting your time fighting this process. You do not want to do this as their customer service is not great. We had this accident once for about 10 seconds of music I stuck at the end of one of my shows to get it to the exact time length I wanted. It was a short use of something in the public domain. I'm an artist and a creator and respect my fellow creatives greatly. I would never take something that is not mine. It proved to be a good learning moment and an even better accident. There was no arguing with them so I immediately recut the show, editing out that 10 seconds of music and putting in my own in its place. I uploaded the updated copy. Eventually they were happy and got off my buns. Their process was funky and it didn't really know how to deal with how I managed the update though (which was odd since it was a simple update). After some time dealing with the customer service people in the legal department though several email chains it got sorted out fully. They did the right thing. They agreed my launched episode was fine, and it remained actively available. Know that if you put anything up that they think is not yours their technology will find it and remove it and you could be blackballed from being able to use the service at all. Be forewarned. Even small accidents matter so avoid the problem.

You can also set up and distribute your podcast show on other platforms if you choose but at the time of this publication it is not required to reach most of the world with your show. You must, of course, review and accept any terms of service required by the directories you set up accounts with. Verify your listing, checking each directory to confirm your podcast episodes appear correctly.

Avoid limiting the directories you choose to the ones you like and know only or because they are your favorites. Most of your new listeners will find you where they prefer to get their podcasts, not where you want to send them. After we list our podcast links to the major directories we always also say "and available everywhere you get your podcasts" so we capture even more new listeners.

After submitting a new episode on any directory be aware that it can take a few hours or more, sometimes up to several days to process and list your show and episodes. You might want to get in the habit of uploading new episodes early in the day. It is like being first at the gym and getting the machines. If you wait until later in the morning when the crowd gets there you are stuck in a queue. Sometimes this can be a long time.

For the podcast The Naughty Librarian 'TNL' the crew gets up very early each Wednesday to drop the podcast everywhere or schedules it early on the accounts where this is an option. This ensures the episode is live everywhere as soon as possible on the day we promise each new episode will be available. Listeners need consistency from you if they are going to stick with your show. Even if the technology is the reason it does not drop, it is ultimately you who has failed them.

To summarize where we recommend you set up and maintain accounts at a minimum to distribute your show into the world, you want to have three accounts: One with RSS, one with Apple Podcasts, and one with Spotify for Creators. These three accounts in aggregate currently distribute your show widely and provide a meaningful picture of your total, worldwide analytics since they each have reasonably good data you can use to gauge your show growth and listenership. Technology is always changing and smaller companies are often starting and closing, but these are enormous businesses that are likely here to stay. Once you're set up on these three major directories your podcast reaches most of the global podcast listening audience and probably will continue to in the future.

Interestingly, the happy part of the accidental use of copyrighted music that I solved quickly by adding my own original music instead was that I started to take this approach whenever I needed a bit of filler or wanted something distinct in the soundtrack. By doing this–just to avoid any copyright ownership concerns technology could flag that would need sorted out–people have reached out asking about it and seeking more. I do not have plans to become a rock star but I've seen weirder things in life.

CHAPTER 9
Sick Killer Results
Words Become Gold

A metric is a quantifiable measure used to track, assess, and evaluate the performance, progress, or health of a business or project like a podcast over time. It is a simple number of some kind that helps show how well a company or activity is doing and can show whether it is improving or getting worse over time. Metrics are the raw numbers that are quantifiable. Analytics involves analyzing those metrics. Analytics turn that raw data into actionable insights for strategy. When you know it, you can grow it.

Quirky to podcasting is that you are the only one on earth who will know exactly how well you are doing with your show. No other company or person ever gets to see all of your podcast metrics and your overall success unless you show them. You are the only one who sees all the data and the whole story. There are a few reasons for this.

One is that people consume podcasts differently. Most listeners do not download the episodes. I rarely do. Many downloads can be automatic and are not necessarily ever listened to. Some listeners can listen to your podcast or excerpts of it directly on your social media platforms or website. Some of the directories your podcasts appear in claim they can tell you the total downloads and listeners of your podcast everywhere, but they can't. This is another reason you want to have separate accounts that you control and only you can log into and see. Your business, and growing your business, is your business.

Only you can see your combined social media activities, monthly paid subscribers, sales from calls, emails, and DM funnels like those you can generate on LinkedIn and in other places. Only you see your profit reports at the end of each month (unless you become a publicly traded company and if that has happened you have really made it, congratulations!).

If you set up and monitor your activities as set out in this book you will have a good picture of your podcast audience size and growth over time and how much money you are making from your show. The combined numbers show you how well you are actually doing in terms of attracting and retaining listeners, generating revenue from your website and other revenue streams you set up, and influencing people with your chosen tactics. No one else will ever have that total knowledge unless you give it to them. You will have the power of the content, its impact, its growth and how to monetize it as a result. You should take screenshots every time you log into one of your accounts and see a strong number of any kind. Save it so you can show potential advertisers when you are pitching to them. It is also fun to post some of these where you want to attract new listeners and advertisers. Sometimes a great review is enough to send a new listener or advertiser to your show to check it out.

As mentioned in the introduction, this podcast started after I completed my MBA and flew to LA to spend time with my terminally ill friend. I threw it together as a diversion project after meeting some great minds at a local writers' group. It was just supposed to be for fun and it did not even have a built out website until half way through the first season (and honestly not a good one until the second season) when I realized it was becoming something big by analyzing the data. Sponsors who are dropping large amounts of money to partner with you and get in front of your listeners expect a professional website and online presence everywhere you are. Meet the moment with the right quality in all that you do.

The podcast show The Naughty Librarian "TNL" was not vulgar. It denounced censorship at a time when attempts to silence creative voices like Jimmy Kimmel were occurring.[1] It drew in guests who are some of the world's greatest and most accomplished authors including Pulitzer Prize winning authors, bestselling authors, celebrity authors, and more. It was about meeting authors and learning about their stories and the stories they tell.

In the first year of starting this podcast, even with taking months off between each season–which so many people say you cannot and should not do but we did because we are in charge and we are naughty–the podcast The Naughty Librarian "TNL" literally took off like wildfire. We grew rapidly, gaining over 95,000+ listeners in 23 countries and 153 cities and growing at last count. All with zero marketing spend and a customer acquisition cost (CAC) of zero. All with word-of-mouth. We blew past the 100,000 listener mark around the year end. All that in the first year.

Some fun screenshots of this growth we captured and shared:

Listeners in 153 Cities By Location

1   Reuters. (2025, September 26). Kimmel ratings give late-night TV a bright spot. Reuters. https://www.reuters.com/business/kimmel-ratings-give-late-night-tv-bright-spot-2025-09-26/

PODCAST: THE NAUGHTY LIBRARIAN "TNL"
AVAILABLE EVERYWHERE YOU GET PODCASTS

Podcast Ranking #180 on Apple Podcast Charts

Apple Podcasts Charts - United States - Entertainment News

THE NAUGHTY LIBRARIAN "TNL". Alexander J. Loudon. 180. Envinadas. Envinadas. 181. Feuds: Power, Pride, and Payback. Caloroga Shark Media. 182. Your Aunties ... <u>See more</u>

It got so big so fast that at one point we ranked on Apple Podcasts before knowing that was something that could even occur! Check this screenshot out:

Podcast Ranking Breaks Top 150 on Apple Podcast Charts!

Based on the above results that had NO marketing budget we clearly tapped into something that people wanted, like oil to a landman in Texas.

My goal on the podcast was simple. It was to give amazing authors a spotlight to send their voice and creativity out to the world further. We were sharing the truth and getting their truth out. It resonated. As one guest in season 2 so graciously told me:

The Naughty Librarian podcast had that lightning a bottle factor Hollywood loves. The metrics were showing it.

Whatever your niche and however you choose to promote it and build it, you will get some growth. You want to capture these numbers, the metrics that observably state this growth so you can show potential advertisers, sponsors and partners you are selling to. This helps to convince them that they have an opportunity to get in on the ground floor and reach people they want to through your podcast, whether it is from buying an advertisement that goes in an episode or by sponsoring an event, or something else.

Increased listeners can mean increased earnings and profits if you capture the proof and tell others about it. These visuals become your sales tools.

My audience growth led to curiosity and more interest on my LinkedIn platform. When I was able to post (not often but some to start), it went very well. Some of the world's most successful professional people and world leaders became connections and listeners, which in turn enabled more selling opportunities, more opportunities to find great guests, and more growth overall. Look what happened with one good post about an episode.

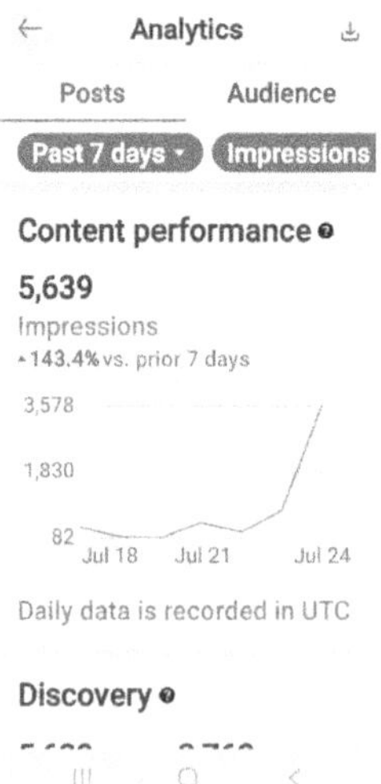

Metrics and analytics are great. Honestly in the beginning I rarely had time to look because it was so much work trying to figure out what I was doing next to deliver each next episode, showrunning, and doing every task of the entire project. I did not have a book like this at the start of my podcasting journey to teach me, help me solve problems. I was making choices and learning as I went constantly. I was forging the new ground. It was exhilarating, and busy!

If I want to break it down into fun, nerdy math numbers and percentages, the following can be said about this first year. With 4 months off between seasons and posting episodes these numbers are actually, technically conservative.

Podcast Listener Size Growth, Year 1

Listeners: 9,999,900% annual growth — this reflects going from 1 listener to 100,000 of them in one year.

To calculate Percentage Increase of your listeners first subtract the final value minus starting value, then divide that amount by the absolute value of the starting value and multiply by 100 to get the percent increase. If the percentage is negative, it means there was a decrease and not an increase. Dislike doing the math longhand? A great resource is online at www.calculatorsoup.com.

Cities with Listeners Growth

Cities: 14,900% annual growth — this reflects expanding from 1 city to over 150 cities in one year.

Countries with Listeners Growth

Countries: 2,200% annual growth — this reflects expanding from 1 country to over 23 countries in one year.

Our naughty cheeky factor growth? Off the charts! Heck, we have people who run countries and the world's biggest businesses among others who follow me on LinkedIn and listen to the show. When my podcast hit #134 on the charts above my friends at TMZ I posted a cheeky, fun photo on LinkedIn teasing them that we ranked higher than they did that week. It was done with love, of course. I'm genuinely humbled and appreciative of this initial success.

Learn to love metrics and take screenshots when you see anything that shows growth of your show. These numbers will become your best friend. They provide objective, measurable ways to view your words as they turn into gold. When that happens and the growth comes you can up your professional game to take it even further. You can insert these screenshots of your success into your sales tools you use to communicate with professional sales and marketing team members in larger companies. You can use them to develop your media kit, rate sheet, promotional short trailers, other short videos and more. That in turn can then lead to even more growth, generating a positive feedback loop. This builds momentum. This is your side hustle podcast well under way!

Be careful not to get addicted to these metrics and outcomes. Staring at a result does not make the result. Do not get into that trap. Check them out then forget about them and move on. You drive looking forward, not in the rearview mirror. The next chapter helps you understand how to slam on the gas pedal.

CHAPTER 10
How to Take Your Podcast to the Next Level
Your New World of Possibilities

Once your podcast is up and growing and you are taking screenshots and using them to make sales and generate revenue from your podcast you want to take your success to the next level. This chapter tells you how to do that. It provides more detailed information on how to make sales using standard industry practices available to successful podcasters. It explains information on tools professional teams use as they scale up their operations in this, still forming, area of the entertainment industry.

Growing your audience and your profits takes patience, consistency and time. Always drop every episode promised on time or communicate to your audience if you cannot. Always complete the daily, weekly, and monthly promotional steps outlined in your 12 Month Marketing and Social Media strategy and if you find it is untenable it is ok to return to it, update it now that you know what might be more realistic for you, and use that updated plan. Always keep up with the non-revenue generating tasks of daily business which include basic bookkeeping and reports and paying required bills, so the business foundation for making money stays strong underneath you. Equally important, always care about your mental health and physical wellness. There is no you as a podcaster if you have nothing to give. The most successful business people create a balance where they are thriving in business and happy and emotionally alive outside of business. With that mindset, you can take your business and podcasting operations as far as you want to. No one can cancel your show but you. Time is a key ingredient to success.

As podcasting goes from 'experimental' advertising opportunities for businesses large and small to becoming normalized as part of standard brand media plans with real value adding to their marketing mix performance[1] your revenue opportunities continue to increase. It will continue to become easier to reach out to companies directly with your advertising and partnership offers and have them say yes. They will understand the value. Remember it is new to a lot of them as well, buying directly from influencers. They will love the reach they get by partnering with you for a fraction of what they have been spending elsewhere. This rising tide will lift all boats (except for the people getting cut out of the middle).

With resilience you forge forth as a side hustle podcaster, making it bigger, making it better and making it your own big entrepreneurial success. When a business is doing well and grows larger it is called 'scaling.' You are now scaling your side hustle podcast.

There are no single formed Standard Operating Procedures (SOPs) or Standard Industry Practices (SIPs) in podcast advertising sales yet but some are emerging. Some podcasters who become influencers negotiate flat rates for partnerships and other sponsorship deals with

1   Shepherd, I. (2025, November 7). The podcast boom is just getting started for brands. Forbes. https://www.forbes.com/sites/ianshepherd/2025/11/07/the-podcast-boom-is-just-getting-started-for-brands/

other companies and their brands, including 360 deals (a strategic collaboration where the two brands integrate across multiple touchpoints–marketing, content, product, events, and distribution—to create shared value throughout the entire customer journey). Others use metrics and formulas to determine worth and set prices. Whatever you do, do not undervalue yourself.

When dealing with established marketing departments who spend billions of dollars annually to promote their products and services, long established sales tools called a "Pitch Deck" and a "Rate Card" are expected. These have been used in traditional media for a long time and they have been given a digital face lift in the podcasting era. They are an essential part of your sales process. So before you have someone ask to see your pitch deck and ask for your rate card, here is the information you need to know to generate them.

Pitch Deck

When asked for my pitch deck as I started selling more ads for the podcast The Naughty Librarian I made a video for it. Most people create a pitch deck as a physical document, or a digital document such as a PDF. Some make a power point presentation. Everyone prefers being entertained over homework so try to make a short, succinct video if you can. Generating a video that looks and feels like a movie trailer shows your creativity and your numbers. After all, you are ultimately selling them on you as a successful creative person in the entertainment business. If you don't have the time and skills to make a slick video a clear, well summarized PDF document will suffice. One page is the best option if you are creating a document unless it is a complex pitch. They can always ask questions from your summary content if they are interested and you have provided enough sufficient detail in the summary that entices them. You can have supplementary attachments at the ready to provide them as well. Know your numbers and your business. Avoid death-by-power point where at all possible as it left with the dinosaurs.

There are different ways to share this video once it is ready. Even a short video can be too large a file to attach with an email. Not everyone uses the same drop box type technology and you do not want to force someone to open a new account to view your video and pitch.

You can put the file in drive and share the link by emailing it to them or enabling shared access with their email. This can be effective, however if it goes through different people on the team or different departments it can cause the process to stall and get awkward, slowing it down. You will have to grant access for each new person who wants to look at the file. You want a fast sales process where the company is excited and happy and everyone gets to "yes" quickly.

One way you can share it that enables a whole team to access it easily is by uploading your MP4 video pitch deck to YouTube and in the process mark it private, with link only, instead of public. That way only those individuals with the link can find it and see it. You can email or text the link to one member of the team during your DM funnel or sales call and they can easily share it with everyone in their company who needs to see it to make the decision to buy what you are offering. This is an excellent way to share the large video pitch deck to all of your prospects easily with little effort on your part. It eliminates the need for everyone to have to use the same large file sharing technology and platform. Everyone knows about YouTube and can access this private video quickly with the generated link. You can also put something in the description that is generic enough to be read by every prospect you send to it yet exciting enough that if they read it they will learn the benefits to advertising or partnering with you. When done with it or updating it you can just delete it and repeat the process with an updated file and link.

Once you have a company interested in buying advertising space from you, you get to tell them the price. Since it is constantly updating as your success continues to rise, the companion tool that you should create that goes with your Media Kit is called a Rate Card. Like a menu at a chain restaurant that lists items and their costs (and has market price for lobster) a rate card shows what is for sale and at what price. It regularly updates to reflect supply, demand and availability of the offerings. This is proprietary, confidential business information. Typically, you do not want to make it public. You want to present its contents only to prospects who are interested in purchasing. Include the date and indicate that prices are subject to change.

A rate card is an essential tool utilized by marketing and advertising agencies, PR agencies, and other businesses such as independent business podcasters, to establish and confidentially communicate the current standard pricing structure for various products and services available for purchase. This comprehensive list serves as a reference point during pricing negotiations with clients.

Within the rate card, a podcaster meticulously outlines the costs associated with their range of services and products, such as creative development of ads of various lengths and ad placement in episodes, and more. By clearly defining the rates for each item for sale, the rate card enables the podcaster to provide clients with a transparent breakdown of current items available and their costs, fostering trust and facilitating informed decision-making.

Moreover, the rate card plays a crucial role in maintaining consistency across the podcaster's pricing strategies. It serves as a reference for internal teams as these departments grow, ensuring that all members are aligned and adhere to the established pricing structure. This consistency not only streamlines your operations but also enhances your podcast show's reputation as a reliable and professional partner in the advertising industry to prospects.

For podcasting professionals new to the advertising field, understanding the concept of a rate card is vital. It equips your sales team (which just might be you still, or might be an entire crew you have hired by now) with the knowledge and vocabulary necessary to engage in pricing discussions with potential purchasers, enabling them to negotiate effectively and advocate for fair compensation for your advertisements, partnerships, sponsorships, licensing opportunities, and whatever else you have to offer.

In summary, a rate card is a comprehensive document traditionally utilized by marketing and advertising companies that podcasters now also use to establish standard pricing for their products, services and anything else that is for sale. It shows the prices and they are subject to change.

How do you know where to set the prices for this menu of your amazingness? For some, a flat rate works. For others, one trend that is emerging to determine what to charge is by using something called the Cost Per Mille (CPM). This is explained next.

CPMs and Pricing

Of the industry trends that are emerging to sell ads on your podcast, CPMs to set pricing for rate cards is becoming a thing. CMP stands for Cost Per Mille (or thousand), a standard advertising metric where advertisers pay for every 1,000 downloads (impressions) of a podcast episode featuring their ad. This is an important concept because it provides a clear, easy to understand and communicate way you can set up and price your podcast advertisements that are for sale. This is a useful way you can get started if you have no idea how to set prices. You are in the big leagues now, dealing with some companies that have billion dollar marketing budgets. You want some of that spend and this is a way to convince them to take a chance on you and get it. It is professional. Here is what you need to know to sell ad space using CPMs.

To clarify a point, in podcasting, impressions measure how many times an episode or ad is shown or served, while downloads count how many times listeners actually request or download the episode. As mentioned before, people may not download episodes but may listen one or more times (impressions). People may or may not follow or subscribe to you anywhere to be loyal listeners and repeat listeners either.

If you sell ads per episode you can sell 1 ad per each 10 or 15 minutes of podcast content, which is standard with up to 7 ads per podcast at the most. Any more than this and listeners will start to go away and not come back. That said, making your podcast longer just to sell ads will also bore listeners who have busy lives so be careful to avoid choosing this route to make more money. If you are having that problem, good! Hire support crew and make more podcasts to sell more ads. You are hitting amazing levels of success!

For video, if you have reached the point where it makes strategic sense that your video is going along with your podcast and it is not just a placeholder (or if it is in one tier of subscribing that still has ads, for example), the sweet spot for this is a bit different, with only 2 ads per

30 minutes. That audience is less tolerant. For a combination of audio with placeholders and video you can choose and either find the middle or choose something else. By trying you will get a feel very quickly for what works and what does not. Be ready to pivot from a plan that is losing you listeners and advertisers. Remember we are in the early days of the gold rush and it is all up for grabs. There are still no rules, only good options. Your monthly listeners and sales results will guide you. It is an imperfect science, deciding how much you can charge as you grow. Your price should go up as your show gains a larger audience.

Podcast advertising rates measured as Cost Per Mille (CPM) are influenced by multiple factors. Key determinants include the podcast's track record and proven performance, the level of bespoke or customized content required, and the value advertisers place on reaching a specific audience. Personal brand or celebrity status can also command higher rates, as can the platform or channel used, since some channels—like LinkedIn—offer more influential and higher-quality audiences than others, such as TikTok. Success also depends on understanding the advertiser's knowledge of the medium and maintaining fairness in dealings, since reputation matters in long-term business relationships. Ultimately, keep in mind that effective podcast ad sales require continuous research, testing, and engagement to see what strategies work best.

Example of CPM Pricing

Ad Type	CPM Range	Description
Programmatic ad	From about $1 to up to $20	One they provide
Host-read ad	$21 - $35	That is you speaking their copy that either they make or you do, or some mix of both
Branded content	$35 - the sky	Includes all kinds of branded content and 360 deals from sponsored webinars. custom episodes with embedded (including stealth) content, series, live events, and more

This chart suggests pricing CPMs for podcast ads varying by type: programmatic ads provided by the advertiser range from about $1 to $20, host-read ads, where you deliver the copy either created by the advertiser or yourself (or a mix), typically range from $21 to $35, and branded content starts at $35 and can go much higher, encompassing sponsored webinars, custom episodes with embedded or stealth content, series, live events, and other 360-degree deals.

A simple example using this structure is if a podcast has 50,000 impressions in a month and a $25 CPM cost per download, 1000 downloads. The simple math is 50,000 divided by 1000 (which is 50) multiplied by $25.

So 50 times $25 = $1,250. You get $1,250 per commercial.

If you have four ad slots in a half hour episode that is a beautiful $5,000. Not bad for half an hour of speaking and another hour of editing and posting.

If you have a podcast that is already getting 50,000 impressions and you are not making this money yet you need to up your game on the marketing side of your business. There is money sitting on the table waiting for you. Use this CPM formula to sell ads to prospects. You have done most of the work to earn it already!

360 Brand Partnerships

A 360 brand partnership, introduced above, can be priced based on what you feel you are worth when negotiating the deal. This is a strategic collaboration where two or more brands integrate across multiple touchpoints—marketing, content, product, events, and distribution—to create shared value throughout the entire customer journey. That is a dream connection you and your brand can make with another business, the bigger the better. This is striking gold with your podcast!

The way to find your price is simple. How big are you and how much do you think someone will pay? You might have a great niche so getting in front of your audience will have more value than some other podcasts might offer.

Always start high but not unreasonably so. So you have room to negotiate. If you start too low you never know how much more you could have obtained in the transaction. You will know if you are too high because no one will be nibbling. Come back to earth and try again.

In conclusion please remember that pricing anything is like pricing antiques. Sand in a bottle or an old brown table could be worth millions. What it costs and ultimately the value it has is always what the market will bear, in other words, if you can get a buyer for what you are selling and at a price you set then that is what it costs and is what it is worth. You are in charge and have the power to set it and get it, or not. Podcast advertising sales is a very creative opportunity to gain wealth in exchange for value you have created for another company with your audience of listeners that no one else has. Never sell yourself short.

With your riches you can save, invest, and spend. It is always nice to support those who are less fortunate with sustainable programs offering opportunities you create yourself or contribute to through reputable, established charities. If you are excited that you can finally buy that sports car of your dreams, read on influencer. You truly are a rock star now.

CHAPTER 11
Don't Be a Broke Rock Star

Financial Success and Wealth Health

If you save and invest money, you can turn it into a lot of money. You can then live off of the interest and never have to work another day in your life ever again. You can snowboard or draw or chase kangaroos–whatever the fun is for you when you are not required to attend work or school.

A smart side hustle that grows your wealth creates money to make more money for you. You will not get to a rich retirement at any age by just putting it in a savings account at a bank or spending it.

If you want to have enough money to live comfortably for the rest of your life–and the amount required varies markedly among people–you need to make enough money to save it and grow it in an investment account that earns you sufficient returns you can live off of. Most podcasters will not make millions, but hundreds of thousands of dollars of profit is not out of reach or unrealistic if you work consistently and smartly and keep at it. Then you want to invest your profits to grow your personal wealth faster so you can get to the part with your feet up by the pool and shrimp on the barbie.

Even if you are one of the few podcasters who wins the equivalent of the lottery by getting a multimillion dollar contract, you want to be smart with your wealth. If you make any profit at all from podcasting, don't be a broke rock star and spend it.

True story number one: I once worked with a guy who won the lottery, a large 6 figure amount. He bought a house and a boat, a divorce, and spent it all. He ended up with no savings. When I met him he was making about $40,000 a year with lots of overtime in an unpleasant, unsafe work environment with bad hours including overnight shifts and forced double shifts. He was a bit grumpy and people around him did not particularly like him. He was a jerk. Do not be that guy.

The moral of that story is that if you come into a large amount of money podcasting you need to earn enough money from that first pile of profits to live off of it without having to take another crummy job again or having to succeed in another side hustle again. You want to save and invest it, and live off of the interest if you are not already wealthy.

Everyone has a different amount of money they want or need to receive annually to live sufficiently well. As we age sometimes life causes us to have bills we do not have when we are younger and do not expect, including unplanned medical bills. It is just a reality of life. A friend I knew ate healthy, exercised, did not take drugs, was happy and healthy living a comfortable, adventurous life and was killed by her body before she turned 40. The medical bills for her family, with insurance, were sizable. Others experience car accidents they do not cause, have parents who get sick, children who are born with extra needs, or have any number of expensive life changing events. Life is full of unplanned, costly events. You want to grow your nest egg to cover them now, and tomorrow.

This short, important chapter gives you a game plan for how to approach generating sufficient wealth to retire. It encourages you to not be that jerk who won the lottery, spent it, and had to take an unpleasant job to pay the bills. While I value seeing my elders throughout my day in the grocery or retail store, gas station, or gym, I do feel some of them would rather be elsewhere and know often they are there because they need to work to earn a wage and do not have sufficient savings to retire. Governments are spending their way out of any social security safety net available at present and you could conceivably get nothing out of what you put in, so that cannot be counted on either. Before social security programs, if people could not earn they would die. Those days, conceivably, can return.

Let's say you need $100,000 to live in each 12 month period. To get that $100,000 per year in income with the reasonable expectation you can earn 2.5 percent on your investments, you'll need $4 million saved ($100,000 /. 025 = $4 million).[1] This is simplistic, to make a point. People live longer and returns are not guaranteed.

True story number two: This is an actual screenshot of one of my investment accounts taken this month. The 'basis' is what it costs me and the gain is the profit. Not bad for a few clicks. This is why you want to invest the money you make instead of buying a new sports car immediately. You can live off of the interest and get the car as well, which is a much better plan.

Here is the important part closer up:

My first career was in investment banking so I use safe leverage plays to grow my portfolio, including trading options. The gains are not

---

1   Massachusetts Mutual Life Insurance Company. (2025, February 28). Interest-only retirement: How to live off investment interest in retirement. MassMutual Blog. https://blog.massmutual.com/retiring-investing/interest-only-retirement

always as good as this one, but sometimes they are. Risk can be controlled for. You are not expected to learn to become a stock broker, but you could hire a good one who can do it for you.

There are a lot of ways to grow wealth and a bank account earning interest is never one of them, nor is spending it all.

Adding to your team as your wealth increases, you should consider hiring a good money manager or financial planner. I knew a financial planner who took the test and then never worked again but married a billionaire. I wouldn't trust her with my money but would fly to the Amazon on her private jet with her while her husband spends time with the new mistress (did I mention she started out as the mistress?). Find someone to grow your money with you who has credentials, experience and walks their talk. Start small when folding in a financial professional to ensure they provide you with the communication and results you seek.

So save, and invest. Then get the car, the crib, the adventures and the clothes from the returns your larger pot of money generates as you comfortably retire.

Then you do not have to be a broke rock star when your podcast is over. And one day it will be.

As you were.

CHAPTER 12
The Future for
The Naughty Librarian
"TNL"

Flying with New Wings

With the final episode last season, an historic and incredible look into the world and mind of one of the world's greatest poets, Diane Seuss, there developed an increased appreciation of what was occurring with this podcast. It became bigger than any one person involved with it. We were literally making history along with having fun and creating enjoyable, educational entertainment others were consuming with pleasure in increasing numbers.

Emboldened, we reached out to everyone we wanted to who had one or more books out in the world. Did we think we could get Oprah? Did we really think J.K. Rowling would say yes and grant us 30 minutes of her time to talk all things Potter and beyond? Did we actually believe Keanu would hop on board and be a guest? Why not? Of course we did.

Maybe not all of them. But some. We still do. (Call me!)

The future of the podcast The Naughty Librarian "TNL" looks bright. As long as we are enjoying it and feel like we are saying something important and useful in an entertaining way, and as long as we see that people still want to guest appear and listen, we will keep bringing it to you. We will still keep taking advertising, sponsorship and partnership money when companies want to give it to us and get in front of our listeners. (Call me!).

Nothing lasts forever so we know we are fortunate to be doing this show and seeing success out of it. It is not just about the numbers. Being part of something that gives to others an becomes a piece of our shared history is a great feeling.

I'm thrilled I get to share it with you, both the podcast and now the business opportunity and approach I stumbled on and found success with in this book, so you too can start and grow your own successful "Side Hustle Podcast." Once you are live let us know. We welcome the opportunity to support you, possibly with follows, likes, reviews, ratings and kindness back.

In closing, I would like to boldly share what the business bank account looked like before the turning point.

Before:

Assets (+):	$108.29
Liabilities (-):	$91.38
Total (=):	$16.91

After? The bank account does not look like that any more lol. I'm done working on my first million. Beyond that, details remain proprietary. As the podcast continues to grow I will continue to quietly support community initiatives that assist others in sustainable ways. In a full circle moment, this is what I have always tried to do, including from the first business that was pivoted from at the start of this adventure. Does the universe have a sense of humor? I guess it does. It sure is naughty!

When one door closes another one opens somewhere. Sometimes

we have to give it a little push with our wings through the wind. Out of the ashes from the fierce burning fire, phoenix takes flight.

The next and final chapter provides you with a guide and steps to get started on your side hustle podcast. It provides your actionable workbook from the chapter contents to implement all you have learned throughout this book. Now it is your turn. Let's hear your voice.

Yesterday called. It is jealous of tomorrow. Go side hustle podcaster you!

CONCLUSION
Your Podcast is Next!
Take It Away!

What are you waiting for? Your couch is ready, standing at attention. Your coffee table is ripe for your great big mug and your adoring fans are eager to listen.

As promised, here is your actionable workbook outlining the major goals from the book and pairing them with tasks and a step ladder with steps for you to complete each item toward your goal of having yourfor you to create your own steps to build out and launch your side hustle podcast business. This is a guide. Set it up anyway you like. Complete the sections with your own information, putting it in your word processing document in the cloud or in a binder, whatever works for you.

Once a goal is completed there is a progress tracker to mark it off, a completion reward (because we all deserve those!), and room to make notes.

Enjoy and good luck!

Workbook

MAJOR GOAL: Create Your Business Plan

☑ TASK TO ACHIEVE GOAL:

Build Company Description

Step Ladder:

Steps to Complete Task:

Step 1: _________________________________

Step 2: _________________________________

Step 3: _________________________________

Step 4: _________________________________

Step 5: _________________________________

TARGET COMPLETION DATE:

PROGRESS TRACKER

☐ Task Completed   ☐ Task In Process

Completion Reward:

____

★ Notes / Reflections:

____

____

____

____

MAJOR GOAL: Create Your Business Plan

☑ TASK TO ACHIEVE GOAL:
Build Market Analysis

Step Ladder:

Steps to Complete Task:

Step 1: _______________________________

Step 2: _______________________________

Step 3: _______________________________

Step 4: _______________________________

Step 5: _______________________________

TARGET COMPLETION DATE:

PROGRESS TRACKER

☐ Task Completed ☐ Task In Process

Completion Reward:

____

⭐ Notes / Reflections:

____

____

____

____

MAJOR GOAL: Create Your Business Plan

☑ TASK TO ACHIEVE GOAL:
Build Organization and Management

Step Ladder:

Steps to Complete Task:

Step 1: _______________________________

Step 2: _______________________________

Step 3: _______________________________

Step 4: _______________________________

Step 5: _______________________________

TARGET COMPLETION DATE:

🚀 PROGRESS TRACKER

☐ Task Completed   ☐ Task In Process

🎁 Completion Reward:

____

⭐ Notes / Reflections:

____

____

____

____

MAJOR GOAL: Create Your Business Plan

☑ TASK TO ACHIEVE GOAL:

Build Products and Services

Step Ladder:

Steps to Complete Task:

Step 1: _______________________________

Step 2: _______________________________

Step 3: _______________________________

Step 4: _______________________________

Step 5: _______________________________

TARGET   COMPLETION
DATE:

PROGRESS TRACKER

☐ Task Completed   ☐ Task In Process

Completion Reward:

____

★ Notes / Reflections:

____

____

____

____

MAJOR GOAL: Create Your Business Plan

☑ **TASK TO ACHIEVE GOAL:**

Build Marketing and Sales Strategy

Step Ladder:

Steps to Complete Task:

Step 1: _________________________________

Step 2: _________________________________

Step 3: _________________________________

Step 4: _________________________________

Step 5: _________________________________

TARGET COMPLETION DATE:

PROGRESS TRACKER

☐ Task Completed   ☐ Task In Process

Completion Reward:

____

★ **Notes / Reflections:**

____

____

____

____

MAJOR GOAL: Create Your Business Plan

☑ **TASK TO ACHIEVE GOAL:**

Build Financials

Step Ladder:

Steps to Complete Task:

Step 1: _______________________________

Step 2: _______________________________

Step 3: _______________________________

Step 4: _______________________________

Step 5: _______________________________

TARGET COMPLETION DATE:

PROGRESS TRACKER

☐ Task Completed   ☐ Task In Process

Completion Reward:

____

★ **Notes / Reflections:**

____

____

____

____

MAJOR GOAL: **Create Your Business Plan**

☑ TASK TO ACHIEVE GOAL:

Build Appendices

Step Ladder:

Steps to Complete Task:

Step 1: _______________________________

Step 2: _______________________________

Step 3: _______________________________

Step 4: _______________________________

Step 5: _______________________________

TARGET COMPLETION DATE:

PROGRESS TRACKER

☐ Task Completed   ☐ Task In Process

Completion Reward:

____

★ Notes / Reflections:

____

____

____

____

MAJOR GOAL: **Create 12 Month Marketing and Social Media Plan**

☑ **TASK TO ACHIEVE GOAL:**

Create 12 Month Marketing Plan

Step Ladder:

Steps to Complete Task:

Step 1: _______________________________

Step 2: _______________________________

Step 3: _______________________________

Step 4: _______________________________

Step 5: _______________________________

TARGET COMPLETION DATE:

PROGRESS TRACKER

☐ Task Completed   ☐ Task In Process

Completion Reward:

____

Notes / Reflections:

____

____

____

____

MAJOR GOAL: Create 12 Month Marketing and Social Media Plan

☑ TASK TO ACHIEVE GOAL:

Make a 30 Day Social Media Plan

Step Ladder:

Steps to Complete Task:

Step 1: _______________________________

Step 2: _______________________________

Step 3: _______________________________

Step 4: _______________________________

Step 5: _______________________________

TARGET COMPLETION DATE:

PROGRESS TRACKER

☐ Task Completed   ☐ Task In Process

Completion Reward:

____

★ Notes / Reflections:

____

____

____

____

MAJOR GOAL: Decide on Gear

☑ TASK TO ACHIEVE GOAL:

Review and select

Step Ladder:

Steps to Complete Task:

Step 1: _________________________________

Step 2: _________________________________

Step 3: _________________________________

Step 4: _________________________________

Step 5: _________________________________

TARGET COMPLETION DATE:

PROGRESS TRACKER

☐ Task Completed   ☐ Task In Process

Completion Reward:

____

Notes / Reflections:

____

____

____

____

MAJOR GOAL: Decide on Branding

☑ TASK TO ACHIEVE GOAL:

Consider and select

Step Ladder:

Steps to Complete Task:

Step 1: _______________________________

Step 2: _______________________________

Step 3: _______________________________

Step 4: _______________________________

Step 5: _______________________________

TARGET COMPLETION DATE:

PROGRESS TRACKER

☐ Task Completed   ☐ Task In Process

Completion Reward:

____

★ Notes / Reflections:

____

____

____

____

MAJOR GOAL: **Decide on Niche**

☑ TASK TO ACHIEVE GOAL:
Review and select

Step Ladder:

Steps to Complete Task:

Step 1: _______________________________

Step 2: _______________________________

Step 3: _______________________________

Step 4: _______________________________

Step 5: _______________________________

TARGET COMPLETION
DATE:

PROGRESS TRACKER

☐ Task Completed   ☐ Task In Process

Completion Reward:

____

★ Notes / Reflections:

____

____

____

____

MAJOR GOAL: **Decide on Podcast Format, Length and Related Details**

☑ **TASK TO ACHIEVE GOAL:**

Review and select

Step Ladder:

Steps to Complete Task:

Step 1: _______________________________

Step 2: _______________________________

Step 3: _______________________________

Step 4: _______________________________

Step 5: _______________________________

TARGET COMPLETION DATE:

PROGRESS TRACKER

☐ Task Completed   ☐ Task In Process

Completion Reward:

____

★ **Notes / Reflections:**

____

____

____

____

MAJOR GOAL: Determine the Plan to Record Your First Episode.

☑ **TASK TO ACHIEVE GOAL:**

Review and list required preparations

Step Ladder:

Steps to Complete Task:

Step 1: _______________________________

Step 2: _______________________________

Step 3: _______________________________

Step 4: _______________________________

Step 5: _______________________________

TARGET COMPLETION DATE:

PROGRESS TRACKER

☐ Task Completed ☐ Task In Process

Completion Reward:

____

★ Notes / Reflections:

____

____

____

____

MAJOR GOAL: Create Podcast Artwork

☑ **TASK TO ACHIEVE GOAL:**
Complete to specifications, on brand and on topic

Step Ladder:

Steps to Complete Task:

Step 1: _______________________________

Step 2: _______________________________

Step 3: _______________________________

Step 4: _______________________________

Step 5: _______________________________

TARGET COMPLETION DATE:

PROGRESS TRACKER

☐ Task Completed   ☐ Task In Process

Completion Reward:

____

⭐ Notes / Reflections:

____

____

____

____

MAJOR GOAL: Create Podcast Thumbnail

☑ TASK TO ACHIEVE GOAL:

Complete to specifications, on brand and on topic

Step Ladder:

Steps to Complete Task:

Step 1: _______________________________

Step 2: _______________________________

Step 3: _______________________________

Step 4: _______________________________

Step 5: _______________________________

TARGET COMPLETION DATE:

PROGRESS TRACKER

☐ Task Completed ☐ Task In Process

Completion Reward:

____

★ Notes / Reflections:

____

____

____

____

MAJOR GOAL: Create Podcast Show Notes

☑ TASK TO ACHIEVE GOAL:
Include keywords, hyperlinks and PSO

Step Ladder:

Steps to Complete Task:

Step 1: _______________________________

Step 2: _______________________________

Step 3: _______________________________

Step 4: _______________________________

Step 5: _______________________________

TARGET COMPLETION DATE:

PROGRESS TRACKER

☐ Task Completed   ☐ Task In Process

Completion Reward:

____

★ Notes / Reflections:

____

____

____

____

MAJOR GOAL: Obtain Copyrights, Trademarks

☑ TASK TO ACHIEVE GOAL:

Determine legal requirements and complete

Step Ladder:

Steps to Complete Task:

Step 1: _______________________________

Step 2: _______________________________

Step 3: _______________________________

Step 4: _______________________________

Step 5: _______________________________

TARGET COMPLETION DATE:

PROGRESS TRACKER

☐ Task Completed ☐ Task In Process

Completion Reward:

____

★ Notes / Reflections:

____

____

____

____

MAJOR GOAL: Obtain Other Required Licenses

☑ **TASK TO ACHIEVE GOAL:**

Determine legal requirements and complete

Step Ladder:

Steps to Complete Task:

Step 1: _______________________________________

Step 2: _______________________________________

Step 3: _______________________________________

Step 4: _______________________________________

Step 5: _______________________________________

TARGET COMPLETION DATE:

PROGRESS TRACKER

☐ Task Completed   ☐ Task In Process

Completion Reward:

____

★ **Notes / Reflections:**

____

____

____

____

MAJOR GOAL: Determine Monetization Strategy

☑ **TASK TO ACHIEVE GOAL:**
Decide and record in business plan

Step Ladder:
Steps to Complete Task:

Step 1: ________________________________

Step 2: ________________________________

Step 3: ________________________________

Step 4: ________________________________

Step 5: ________________________________

TARGET COMPLETION DATE:

PROGRESS TRACKER

☐ Task Completed   ☐ Task In Process

Completion Reward:

____

★ Notes / Reflections:

____

____

____

____

MAJOR GOAL: Determine Sales Survival Strategy

☑ TASK TO ACHIEVE GOAL:

Decide and record in business plan

Step Ladder:

Steps to Complete Task:

Step 1: _______________________________

Step 2: _______________________________

Step 3: _______________________________

Step 4: _______________________________

Step 5: _______________________________

TARGET COMPLETION DATE:

PROGRESS TRACKER

☐ Task Completed   ☐ Task In Process

Completion Reward:

____

★ Notes / Reflections:

____

____

____

____

MAJOR GOAL: Set up/Refresh LinkedIn Profile

☑ **TASK TO ACHIEVE GOAL:**

Complete account on brand and on topic

Step Ladder:

Steps to Complete Task:

Step 1: _______________________________

Step 2: _______________________________

Step 3: _______________________________

Step 4: _______________________________

Step 5: _______________________________

TARGET COMPLETION DATE:

🚀 PROGRESS TRACKER

☐ Task Completed   ☐ Task In Process

🎁 Completion Reward:

____

⭐ Notes / Reflections:

____

____

____

____

MAJOR GOAL: Build Out Website

☑ **TASK TO ACHIEVE GOAL:**

Hire or learn and do, keeping on brand

Step Ladder:

Steps to Complete Task:

Step 1: _______________________________

Step 2: _______________________________

Step 3: _______________________________

Step 4: _______________________________

Step 5: _______________________________

TARGET COMPLETION DATE:

🚀 PROGRESS TRACKER

☐ Task Completed   ☐ Task In Process

🎁 **Completion Reward:**

____

⭐ **Notes / Reflections:**

____

____

____

____

MAJOR GOAL: Decide on Editing Software

☑ TASK TO ACHIEVE GOAL:
Review and select

Step Ladder:

Steps to Complete Task:

Step 1: _______________________________

Step 2: _______________________________

Step 3: _______________________________

Step 4: _______________________________

Step 5: _______________________________

TARGET COMPLETION DATE:

PROGRESS TRACKER

☐ Task Completed   ☐ Task In Process

Completion Reward:

____

★ Notes / Reflections:

____

____

____

____

MAJOR GOAL: Set Up Distribution

☑ TASK TO ACHIEVE GOAL:
Decide and open accounts (RSS, etc)

Step Ladder:

Steps to Complete Task:

Step 1: _______________________________

Step 2: _______________________________

Step 3: _______________________________

Step 4: _______________________________

Step 5: _______________________________

TARGET COMPLETION
DATE:

PROGRESS TRACKER

☐ Task Completed   ☐ Task In Process

Completion Reward:

____

★ Notes / Reflections:

____

____

____

____

MAJOR GOAL: Develop Media Kit

☑ **TASK TO ACHIEVE GOAL:**
Review format options and complete

Step Ladder:

Steps to Complete Task:

Step 1: ___________________________________

Step 2: ___________________________________

Step 3: ___________________________________

Step 4: ___________________________________

Step 5: ___________________________________

TARGET COMPLETION DATE:

🚀 **PROGRESS TRACKER**

☐ Task Completed   ☐ Task In Process

🎁 **Completion Reward:**

____

⭐ **Notes / Reflections:**

____

____

____

____

MAJOR GOAL: Build Rate Card

☑ TASK TO ACHIEVE GOAL:

Based on growth levels.

Step Ladder:

Steps to Complete Task:

Step 1: _______________________________

Step 2: _______________________________

Step 3: _______________________________

Step 4: _______________________________

Step 5: _______________________________

TARGET COMPLETION DATE:

PROGRESS TRACKER

☐ Task Completed   ☐ Task In Process

Completion Reward:

____

★ Notes / Reflections:

____

____

____

____

Acknowledgements

To everyone over 20 years of age who feels like they are too old to be successful in the visual, digital age. To all the jerks I pitched to who ignored me for thirty years, I guess it all worked out. To creatives, everywhere, who keep going, like moths to light, in this awesome, swirling, terrifying and terrible experience called being an artist: I throw a kiss in your general direction and salute you. To regulators, censors and other idiots who aim to suppress creative thought: we don't need you, we don't want you, and you smell. We walk around you and carry a big dictionary. To my small and mighty team, you know who you are. Finally, although it may be a trope, a cliché, overdone…to you, the couch warrior who wants to get ahead in a world that doesn't dole out many opportunities to the little people. Wishing you a strong one — go own it.

How to Stay in Touch with Me

At the time of this writing the following links are active and one way to connect with my team and the show. Note that due to the high-volume of submissions I do not usually look at these personally or engage directly back. The best way to get our attention is to follow one or more of our accounts first and then send a DM saying hello. Thank you in advance for reaching out if you do. Also, some idiot billionaire may purchase and crash any one of these platforms, so the following information is always subject to change. In case of removed accounts, a search of the podcast by name and review of the most recent episode is probably your best way to find current links and other pertinent information.

Podcast Show Website: www.TheNaughtyLibrarian.ca

Social Media Show Links:
IG: https://www.instagram.com/wearetnlofficial/
TIKTOK: https://www.tiktok.com/@wearetnlofficial
Bluesky: https://bsky.app/profile/wearetnlofficial.bsky.social
X: https://x.com/TNLofficial
*YouTube:*https://www.youtube.com/@TheNaughtyLibrarianOfficial
Substack: https://substack.com/@thenaughtylibrarian
IMDB: https://www.imdb.com/title/tt37458178/
LinkedIn: https://www.linkedin.com/in/alexloudonofficial/

Naughty Brats Unite

We support unbiased, independent individuals sharing and storytelling worldwide and global news journalists, reporters, and organizations dedicated to factual reporting. We support listening to every voice. We support free speech. We support global unity and love in our actions and our words. We are not vulgar and that is our choice.

If someone does not feel comfortable with a guest or topic for a show, they are welcome to skip that one. If someone likes a show, they are welcome to tell others and leave a 5-star review! And by the way, thank YOU for checking it out and listening to at least part of an episode so you can then leave a 5-star review which helps us deliver more free content to everyone. Please also reach out and let us know how we can support you once your podcast is in the world! We love returning kindness.

While our goal is to be a family-friendly podcast, some of the guests have opinions, experiences, and creativity that extend beyond the comfort zone of others. The easy solution is that we put a rating on shows if there is content not suitable for all listeners. Should an episode have any themes or content that some people may find offensive or difficult in some way we make it clear in the accurate description and may put an 'explicit' rating on it, to help those who want to avoid such content.

So join the revolution and become a Naughty Brat today! Find the podcast wherever you get your podcasts, start listening and joining the conversation where we are online. We welcome you and are looking forward to hearing from you!

GLOSSARY

360 BRAND PARTNERSHIP

A strategic collaboration where two or more brands integrate across multiple touchpoints–marketing, content, product, events, and distribution—to create shared value throughout the entire customer journey.

ACTUAL-PLAY / ROLE-PLAY FORMAT

Participants play a game (often tabletop RPG) or role-play scenarios and the podcast records the session.

AI AND VOICE SEARCH RANKING

Monitors visibility in AI-driven and voice search results, critical as these discovery channels grow.

AFFILIATE REVENUE

Tracks income from affiliate links or promotions within episodes, showing monetization beyond sponsorships.

ALGORITHM

A set of automated rules and models that analyze your listening behavior (like what you play, skip, or follow) to recommend podcasts and episodes you're most likely to enjoy.

AUDIO DEMOGRAPHIC INSIGHTS

Tracks detailed listener data (age, location, interests) to better target content and marketing.

AUDIENCE SIZE AND GROWTH RATE

Measures the total number of listeners and how fast the audience is expanding over time, indicating popularity and market reach.

AVERAGE DEAL SIZE

The average revenue value per closed sale resulting from podcast-driven leads or campaigns.

AVERAGE REVENUE PER ACCOUNT (ARPA)

Measures average income generated per customer or account acquired through podcast-driven marketing efforts.

AVERAGE REVENUE PER LISTENER (ARPL)

Calculates revenue generated per listener across all monetization channels, showing effectiveness of audience monetization.

AVERAGE SALES CYCLE LENGTH

The average time it takes to close a sale from a podcast-generated lead, helping optimize timing and follow-ups.

BACKLINK VELOCITY

Assesses the rate of new backlinks to the podcast website, reflecting authority and SEO strength.

BANT (IN SALES)

BANT is a sales framework used to qualify prospects by determining whether they have the budget to buy, the authority to decide, a genuine need for the solution, and a defined timeline for making the purchase. All are needed for a sale to be made.

BEHIND-THE-SCENES/PROCESS BREAKDOWN

The host takes listeners through how something was made or how a process works, often in detail.

BITE-SIZED/MINI-EPISODE

Short duration episodes (e.g., under 10-20 minutes) focused on quick tips or insights.

BRAND AWARENESS

Measures how recognizable and memorable your brand is to your target audience. Higher awareness indicates effective marketing reach and positioning in the market.

BRAND AWARENESS LIFT

Assesses increases in brand recognition, search volume, and online mentions driven by the podcast.

CAMPAIGN REACH EFFICIENCY

Measures how effectively campaigns reach the intended audience without wasted impressions or spend.

CASE STUDY/INTERVIEW + ANALYSIS

A guest or host presents a real-world case and then follows with analysis or deconstruction.

CHURN RATE

Measures the percentage of listeners or subscribers who disengage, highlighting retention challenges.

CHURN RATE (SALES PERSPECTIVE)

Tracks the percentage of customers lost over time, showing retention challenges for podcast-driven products or subscriptions.

CO-HOSTED (CONVERSATIONAL)

Two or more hosts engage in a back-and-forth discussion on topics with each other.

CONVERSION RATE

Monitors the percentage of listeners who take a desired action, such as subscribing, purchasing, or joining a mailing list.

CONTENT-ASSISTED CONVERSIONS

Tracks how podcast episodes or related content influence user actions, like purchases or sign-ups.

CONTENT PERFORMANCE

Evaluates blogs, videos, and repurposed podcast content in driving engagement, traffic, and conversions.

COST PER ACQUISITION (CPA)

Calculates the cost to acquire a new customer or lead through podcast-driven marketing, reflecting resource efficiency.

COST PER CONVERSION

Calculates the expense incurred to achieve a specific listener or user action, showing marketing efficiency.

CROSS-PLATFORM PERFORMANCE

Analyzes how podcast content performs on social media, video platforms, newsletters, and blogs, indicating amplification success.

CUSTOMER ACQUISITION COST (CAC) BY CHANNEL

Calculates the cost to acquire a customer specifically through podcast promotions versus other channels.

CUSTOMER ENGAGEMENT METRICS

Tracks interactions such as shares, comments, and social mentions stemming from podcast episodes.

CUSTOMER LIFETIME VALUE (CLV)

Evaluates the total revenue a customer generates over their relationship with the business, linking podcast influence to profitable growth.

CUSTOMER LIFETIME VALUE (CLV) BY SEGMENT

Measures total projected revenue per customer segment acquired via the podcast, helping prioritize high-value audiences.

DM FUNNEL

A structured sequence of direct messages that guides someone from first contact to a specific action, like booking a call, signing up, or making a purchase.

EMAIL OPEN AND CLICK-THROUGH RATES

Measures engagement with marketing emails linked to the podcast, showing effectiveness of messaging.

ENGAGED SESSIONS

Counts visits or listens with meaningful interaction, showing real engagement with podcast content.

ENGAGEMENT RATE

Measures listener interactions—reviews, shares, comments, and social mentions—to gauge connection and community building.

EPISODE COMPLETION RATE

Monitors the percentage of listeners who play episodes to the end, reflecting content engagement.

HYBRID/MIXED FORMAT

A show that combines two or more formats in one episode (e.g., solo commentary + guest interview + panel).

INFLUENCER AMPLIFICATION

Tracks how often industry influencers or partners share or mention the podcast, indicating credibility and reach.

INTERVIEW

One host interviews a guest (or multiple guests) each episode, exploring their insights or experiences.

LEAD GENERATION

Counts qualified leads captured via marketing campaigns linked to the podcast, indicating campaign effectiveness.

LEAD QUALITY

Focuses on the potential of leads generated through the podcast to convert into paying customers.

LEAD-TO-OPPORTUNITY RATIO

Measures how many leads generated from podcast marketing convert into sales opportunities.

LISTENER JOURNEY MAPPING

Analyzes the path listeners take from discovery to engagement to conversion, revealing funnel effectiveness.

LISTENER RETENTION RATE

Shows what percentage of listeners return for new episodes, reflecting content quality, loyalty, and audience satisfaction.

LISTENER Q&A / ASK-ME-ANYTHING

The host answers listener-submitted questions, feedback or challenges in a conversational format.

LISTENER SENTIMENT ANALYSIS

Analyzes reviews, social comments, and feedback to gauge emotional response and audience satisfaction.

LIVE/ON-LOCATION RECORDING

Episodes recorded live with an audience, or on-site in a special location, capturing ambient sound and reactions.

MARKETING QUALIFIED LEADS (MQLS)

Tracks leads deemed ready for sales engagement from podcast-driven campaigns.

MEDIATION/MINDFULNESS GUIDED FORMAT

The host guides listeners through meditation, reflection, or mindfulness experiences.

METADATA

Podcast show metadata is the structured information that describes a podcast, including its title, description, author, category, language, episode list, artwork, and publishing details, used by platforms and directories to organize, display, and distribute the show.

MONTHLY RECURRING REVENUE (MRR)

Tracks predictable revenue generated from subscriptions, memberships, or recurring podcast-related offers.

NARRATIVE/STORYTELLING NON-FICTION

Episodes are structured like audio documentaries or true-story arcs, often heavily produced.

NEWS/CURRENT EVENTS ROUNDUP

Episodes summarise, analyse or comment on recent news, trends or timely events.

OPPORTUNITY-TO-CLOSE RATIO

Percentage of opportunities that successfully convert into sales, indicating efficiency of the sales process.

PAID ADVERTISING PERFORMANCE

Analyzes ROI, click-through rate, and cost metrics for ads promoting the podcast.

PANEL/ROUNDTABLE

A moderator leads a discussion among several hosts and/or guests offering multiple viewpoints.

PIPELINE COVERAGE

Compares the value of deals in the sales pipeline to the target revenue, ensuring sufficient opportunities exist from podcast leads.

PODCAST SEARCH ENGINE OPTIMIZATION (SEO)

The practice of optimizing podcast content and metadata so episodes rank higher and are more discoverable in search engines and podcast platforms.

PODCAST SEARCH OPTIMIZATION (PSO)

The process of optimizing podcast titles, descriptions, and metadata to improve discoverability within podcast apps and search results.

PODFADE

Podfade is industry jargon for when a podcast gradually stops producing new episodes and effectively fades out of existence. It typically happens when creators lose momentum, lose interest in the topic, underestimate the effort required, or fail to maintain a consistent schedule. In short, it's the silent, slow disappearance of a podcast rather than an official cancellation.

PLATFORM BADGE

A platform badge is a digital token, icon, or credential that represents a specific achievement, skill, or status earned on a website, app, or online community. Used for recognition and gamification, these visual symbols often contain embedded metadata that verifies the achievement's authenticity, such as the issuer, criteria, and date earned.

PLATFORM DIVERSITY

Measures listener distribution across apps, streaming platforms, and social channels to optimize reach and reduce risk.

PRIMARY CONVERSION METRICS

Tracks key user actions, like form submissions, newsletter sign-ups, or resource downloads, influenced by the podcast.

REVENUE ATTRIBUTION

Determines which podcast episodes, campaigns, or promotions directly contributed to closed sales and revenue.

REVENUE GROWTH

Tracks the overall increase in income generated by the business due to the podcast, including sponsorships, product sales, subscriptions, and new customer acquisition.

RETURN ON INVESTMENT (ROI)

Compares financial return generated by the podcast to production, marketing, and distribution costs.

SCRIPTED FICTION/AUDIO DRAMA

A fully written and produced fictional story, with actors, sound design and music.

SEASONAL/THEMED SERIES FORMAT

A multi-episode limited run with a cohesive theme, narrative arc or subject matter structured like a mini-series.

SHARE OF VOICE

Compares podcast visibility and influence to competitors in the niche, indicating market presence.

SOCIAL MEDIA ROI

Measures returns from social campaigns that promote or amplify the podcast.

SOCIAL MEDIA REACH AND IMPRESSIONS

Monitors the total number of unique users seeing your content and how often it appears. This helps gauge visibility and audience exposure across platforms.

SOLO (MONOLOGUE)

A single host speaks directly to the audience, sharing commentary, stories or expertise.

SPONSORSHIP AND AD REVENUE

Represents income earned from advertising, sponsorships, or collaborations, indicating commercial success.

STORYTELLING FICTION ANTHOLOGY

Each episode presents a standalone fiction story (rather than a serialized arc) with its own characters and setting.

SUBSCRIPTION GROWTH RATE

Measures growth in premium subscriptions, memberships, or newsletter sign-ups, signaling audience commitment.

THUMBNAIL (PODCAST)

A thumbnail for a podcast is a square cover image (typically 1400×1400 to 3000×3000 pixels, JPG or PNG, RGB color, under 500 KB) used across platforms to visually identify the episode and attract listeners.

TIME-TO-MONETIZATION

Calculates the duration between podcast launch and measurable revenue generation, reflecting efficiency.

TOTAL CHRONOLOGICAL EPISODE NUMBER (TCEN)

The total chronological episode number (TCEN) is the chronological number of the episode regardless of which season it is in and what episode number it has relative to its distinct season. It allows podcasters to label their total episodes in order while allowing for seasons with episodes and breaks in between.

TRAFFIC SOURCES AND VOLUME

Tracks where website visitors come from—organic search, social, referral, paid ads—helping optimize marketing strategy.

UP-SELL AND CROSS-SELL REVENUE

Revenue generated by encouraging existing customers acquired via the podcast to purchase additional or higher-value products.

WIN RATE

Percentage of deals closed successfully out of all opportunities created through podcast marketing efforts.

About "The Naughty Librarian"
Alexander Loudon

Alex J. Loudon is an MBA graduate (2025) and the USA Small Business Administration Woman in Business Champion of the Year, MD (2011). The creator, writer, producer, executive director, host, and savvy marketer of the new hit podcast The Naughty Librarian "TNL," which has had such notable guests as Brian Cuban, Jerry Manas, and Pulitzer Prize–winning poet Diane Seuss, and which, at the time of this book going to press, boasts listeners in over 23 countries and 153 cities, Alex leverages the direct knowledge and secrets gleaned from being behind the mic of this runaway, smash, money-making hit podcast in an easy-to-understand approach with actionable items so you too can immediately get started podcasting and making money from your living room couch.

www.ingramcontent.com/pod-product-compliance
Lightning Source LLC
Chambersburg PA
CBHW050509160726
48003CB00001B/232